Art for a Cure

Paintings and Drawings 2012-2017

Art for a Cure

Paintings and Drawings 2012-2017

Mia Natalie Kamensky

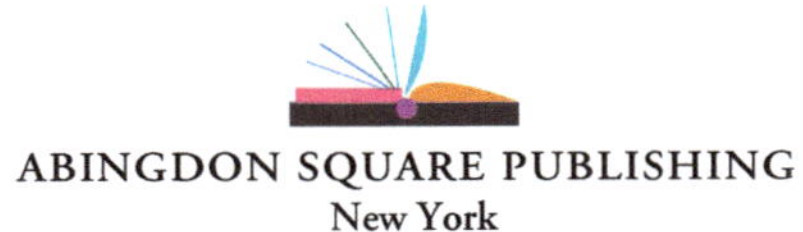

ABINGDON SQUARE PUBLISHING
New York

Art for a Cure
Paintings and Drawings 2012-2017
is published by
Abingdon Square Publishing Ltd.
463 West Street, Suite G122
New York, NY 10014 USA
www.abingdonsquarepublishing.com

Book Design: Abingdon Square Publishing
Front Cover: *On Stage,* Acrylic on paper, 13.5 x 10.5 inches, 2017
Back Cover: *Tree of Life,* Acrylic on paper, 28.5 inches diameter, 2016

The author gratefully acknowledges permission to reproduce and reprint the following material:
"Letter From the Michael J. Fox Foundation for Parkinson's Research" by Liz Diemer
"Letter from Memorial Sloan Kettering Cancer Center" by Tanya M. Trippett, M.D.

ISBN 978-0-9830762-9-2
Library of Congress Control Number: 2018930153

Printed in the United States of America

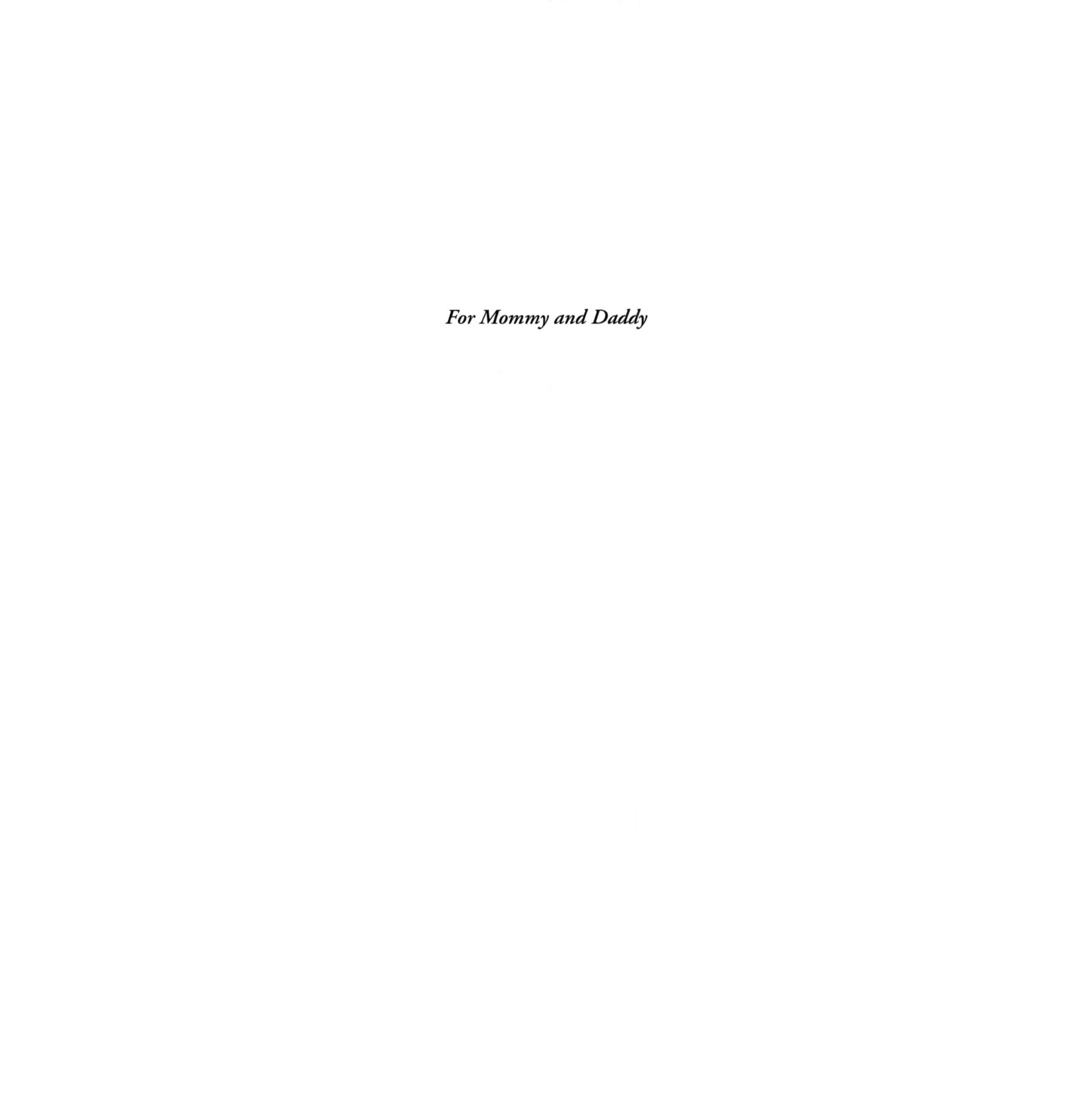

For Mommy and Daddy

Table of Contents

Catalog of Paintings and Drawings

Introduction

**"The artist is nothing without the gift.
But the gift is nothing without the work."**
— *Emile Zola*

You never know what you're going to get when you take on a new art student. Some have talent, some have passion and drive, others are compassionate and sincerely empathetic. Sometimes, it turns out, you are fortunate to be matched with one of those rare ones who possess all of these qualities.

I first met such a student when a company I work for, *Private Picassos,* sent me, as the introductory email stated, "to teach a series of lessons to a talented girl who wants to be challenged and exposed to new materials and skills". Eight year old Mia greeted me at the door already wearing a smock and a schmatta-like headband pulling back her long hair. She was ready to work and work she did. It wasn't long before I realized that Mia possessed "the gift." For a girl so young, I saw she was able to visually translate proper shading and perspective in her drawings, with an innate understanding of spatial relationships. When she painted, I saw she had a natural feel for color, design and composition—all things that can take years to master.

Mia was focused and open-minded at every lesson, and her enthusiasm was inspiring. Moving effortlessly between mediums, she used chalk pastels, charcoal, acrylic and watercolors to create an impressive body of work. Sometimes we worked small, as when she painted a beautiful study of a simple acorn. Sometimes we worked really big, as when she created cherry blossoms inspired by Van Gogh, a work which now fills an entire wall in her dining room. Although many of her pieces have received high recognition in contests and exhibitions, Mia remains sweetly humble and ready for her next challenge.

This book represents not only our many lessons together as teacher and student, but also her giving heart and charitable spirit. These are clearly part and parcel of her artistic gifts. I was not surprised at all when Mia and her mom told me of the intent to use the book's proceeds to help others.

Mia's hard work, talent and loving family have provided her a strong foundation to thrive in the visual arts. I'm honored to have been a part of her journey thus far and grateful for our special friendship, one that I cherish and hold dear. I'm excited to see where Mia's talents take her, and who knows—maybe one day we'll see "Kamenskys" hanging on the walls of galleries and museums around the world!

— Christina Sahr, Art Teacher
December 2017

Artist's Statement

Thank you for supporting my Mitzvah Project!

For as long as I can remember, I have loved to paint. Art has never been just a hobby for me; it has always been part of my identity. The paintings and drawing in this book are pieces I have made over the years beginning when I was in kindergarten. I have learned a lot during my six summers at USDAN, a day camp for the arts, but my amazing art teacher, Chris Sahr, is the one who helps me to continue to develop my skills. She inspires me to be as creative as I can be. Whether it's painting, sketching, squirting acrylics on a pallet, playing music, or even just talking, we always have so much fun. Art has become even more exciting and special to me because of Chris.

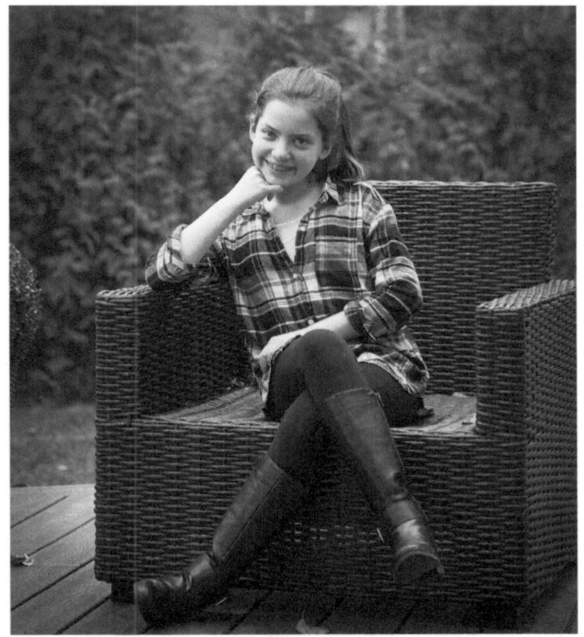

By purchasing this book you are helping to find a cure for two illnesses: Cancer and Parkinson's disease.

I have a personal connection to both causes. My grandpa from Chicago (Papa) and my grandma here in New York (Nah-Nah) both have Parkinson's disease. I have seen how horrible and challenging this condition can be for them as well as for our family. There needs to be a cure. By buying my art book you are helping The Michael J. Fox Foundation for Parkinson's Research find a cure sooner rather than later.

Memorial Sloan Kettering Cancer Center is a special place for my family because they saved my mom's life. My mom is not just my mom. She's my best friend. Way before I was born, when my mom was 13-years-old, she was diagnosed with an advanced stage of Hodgkin's disease, a form of cancer. The doctors in the pediatric department at Memorial Sloan Kettering Cancer Center gave my mom an experimental treatment that they had never tested on a patient with her same disease. This treatment saved her life. Now she is my mom. I am so thankful. That is why I would like to support this hospital – so that kids who are very sick, just like my mom was, can grow up to lead healthy, happy lives.

I'd like to thank my family – Mommy, Daddy, Nah-Nah, Pop, Grammy, Papa, Aunt Michelle, Uncle Josh, Uncle Todd, Uncle Rob, Aunt Debbie, Shayna, Keren, Rebecca, Megan, Jenna, Bari, Ari, Alexis – for their love. And all my friends, for supporting me in everything I do.

Also, I'd like to thank Oron, Marcia and Naftali Tal for their inspiration, Kazuhito Sakuma for his photography, and Andrea Piccolo and Valentina DuBasky for publishing this book and turning my dream into reality.

I hope you enjoy my book as much as I enjoyed creating the art.

— Mia Natalie Kamensky

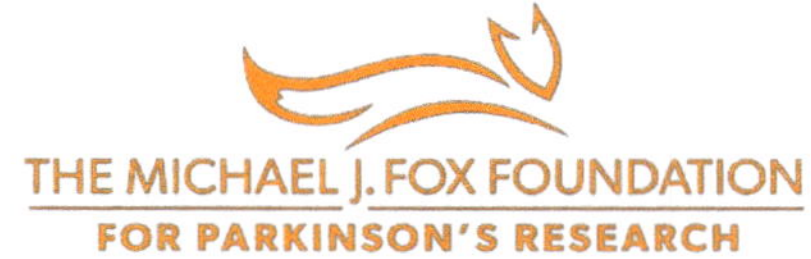

November 20, 2017

Dear Mia,

I am writing this letter to express our enthusiasm, thanks and support for your upcoming Mitzvah Project on February 11, 2018. We are extremely grateful for your commitment to fight Parkinson's disease and are honored that a portion of proceeds from your fundraising will go directly to The Michael J Fox Foundation (MJFF). Thanks to the dedication of community members like you, we believe we will find a cure for the millions of people living with this disease.

Community fundraisers are extremely useful — not only raising funds for research but also galvanizing Parkinson's awareness among family, friends and colleagues. Your activities give hope to others and mobilize desire into action, making progress possible. Your contribution helps move forward The Michael J Fox Foundation's mission to find a cure for Parkinson's disease.

To date, The Michael J Fox Foundation for Parkinson's Research has invested over $750 million in the field with 89 cents of every dollar spent going straight to the research program effort. Furthermore, thanks to the generous support of an anonymous donor, 100% of donations given to MJFF by Team Fox members will go directly to research efforts to help speed a cure.

Since inception, MJFF has maintained an uncompromising pace, inspiring and advancing the most promising research. We strategically target our resources to achieve maximum scientific impact. Our initiatives attract and support established world-class scientists as well as researchers new to the field of Parkinson's. Every day, these research pioneers face the same challenge: Nearly five million people worldwide live with Parkinson's disease. Finding a cure has never been more urgent.

As you help to organize this event and seek sponsorship and support, please note that I would be happy to talk with any of your sponsors about the research we fund or any aspect of the Foundation's mission, should they desire more information.

All the best and thank you again!

Liz Diemer
Director, Team Fox

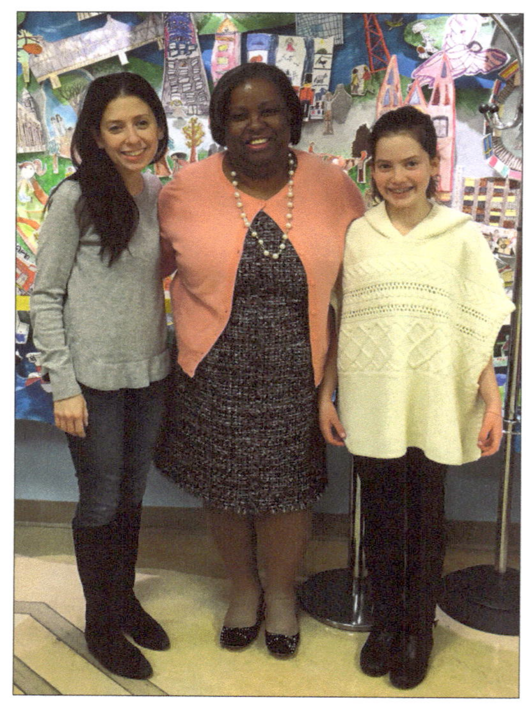

Amy and Mia with Dr. Trippett
of the Memorial Sloan Kettering Cancer Center

Memorial Sloan Kettering
Cancer Center

The Department of Pediatrics at the Memorial Sloan Kettering Cancer Center (MSK) treats more children with cancer than any other hospital in the United States, and leads the world in developing new ways to fight these diseases. While 80 percent of children with cancer are now cured, unfortunately cancer still remains the leading cause of disease-related deaths in young patients. The key to further improving the survival rate is research, and private support has been fundamental to driving critical advances in the field.

Most recently, MSK's Department of Pediatrics has been focused on a variety of research initiatives aimed at ultimately developing more effective, less toxic treatments for our youngest patients. By utilizing capital MSK-IMPACT to perform genomic sequences of all pediatric tumors, we have been able to apply this data to guide new treatment options in the form of drugs that target genetic mutations and spare healthy cells from damage.

In my own work as Director of the Pediatric Oncology Experimental Therapeutics Investigator Consortium (POETIC) Coordinating Center in New York City, the development of biologically targeted therapies for pediatric cancers has seen great progress in recent years, increasing patients' access to promising new agents and clinical trials. The work we've done in the laboratory and its translation to improve the treatment of lymphoma is now being applied to the care of children with other types of cancer.

Now is a time of unprecedented progress in the field of pediatric cancer—and nowhere is this momentum stronger than at MSK. It is very gratifying when I see patients conquer cancer and go on to do well in life. I understand how critical research is to advancing the treatment of cancer, and it is rewarding to know that the investigations I am leading may save the life of a child.

I am deeply grateful to Mia and her family and friends for their commitments to our mission.

Sincerely,

Tanya M. Trippett, M.D.
Associate Attending Pediatrician
Co-Founder & Director, POETIC

Flowers

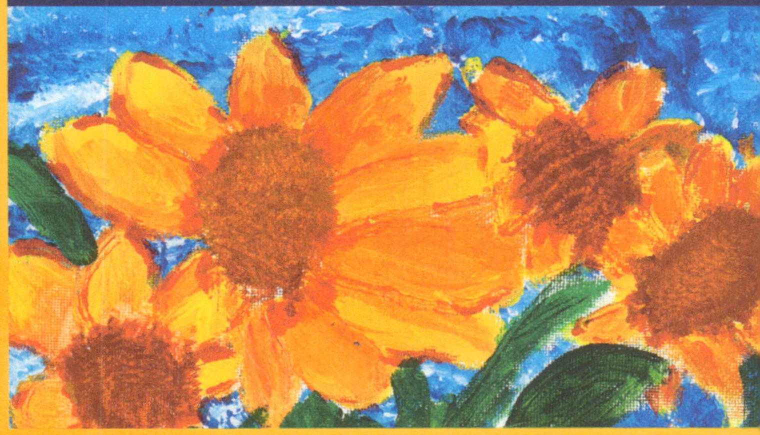

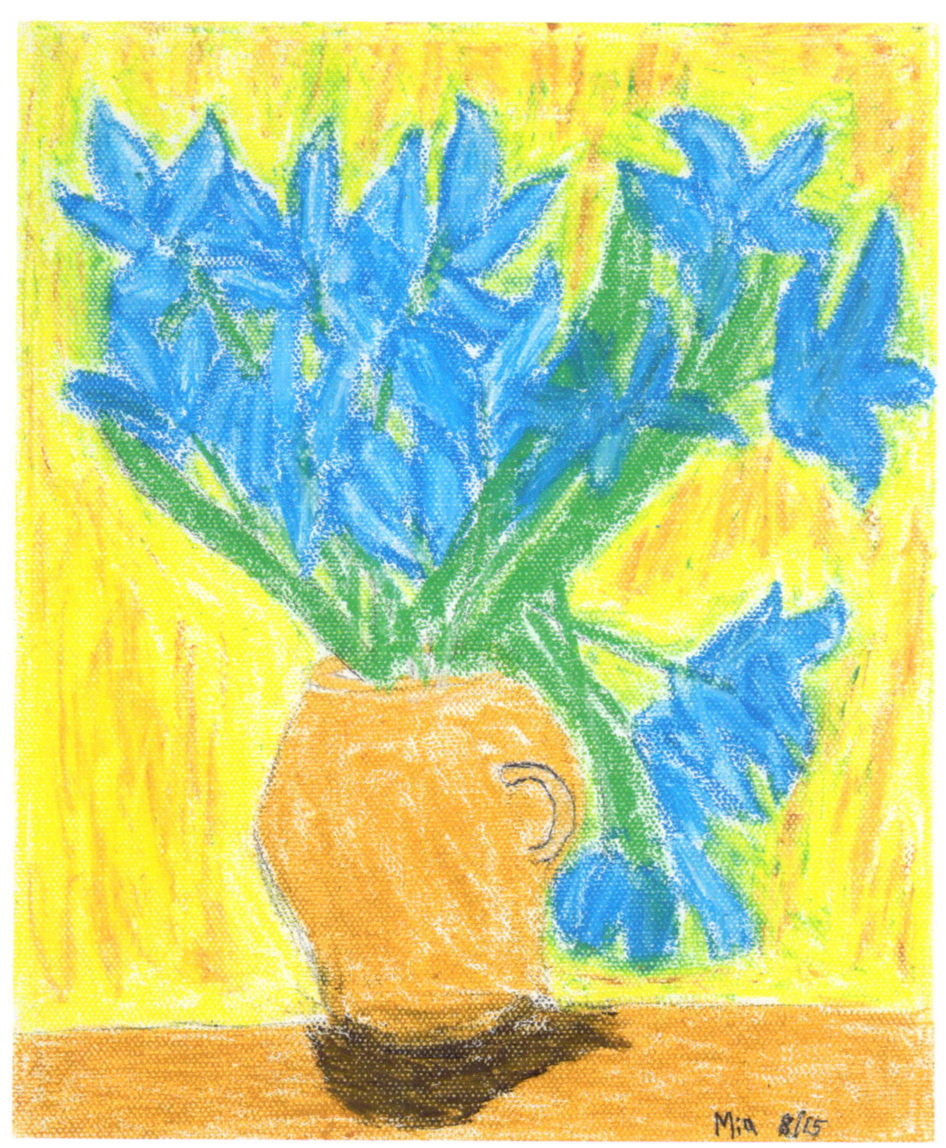

Irises (inspired by Van Gogh)
Oil pastel on canvas, 10 x 8 inches
2015

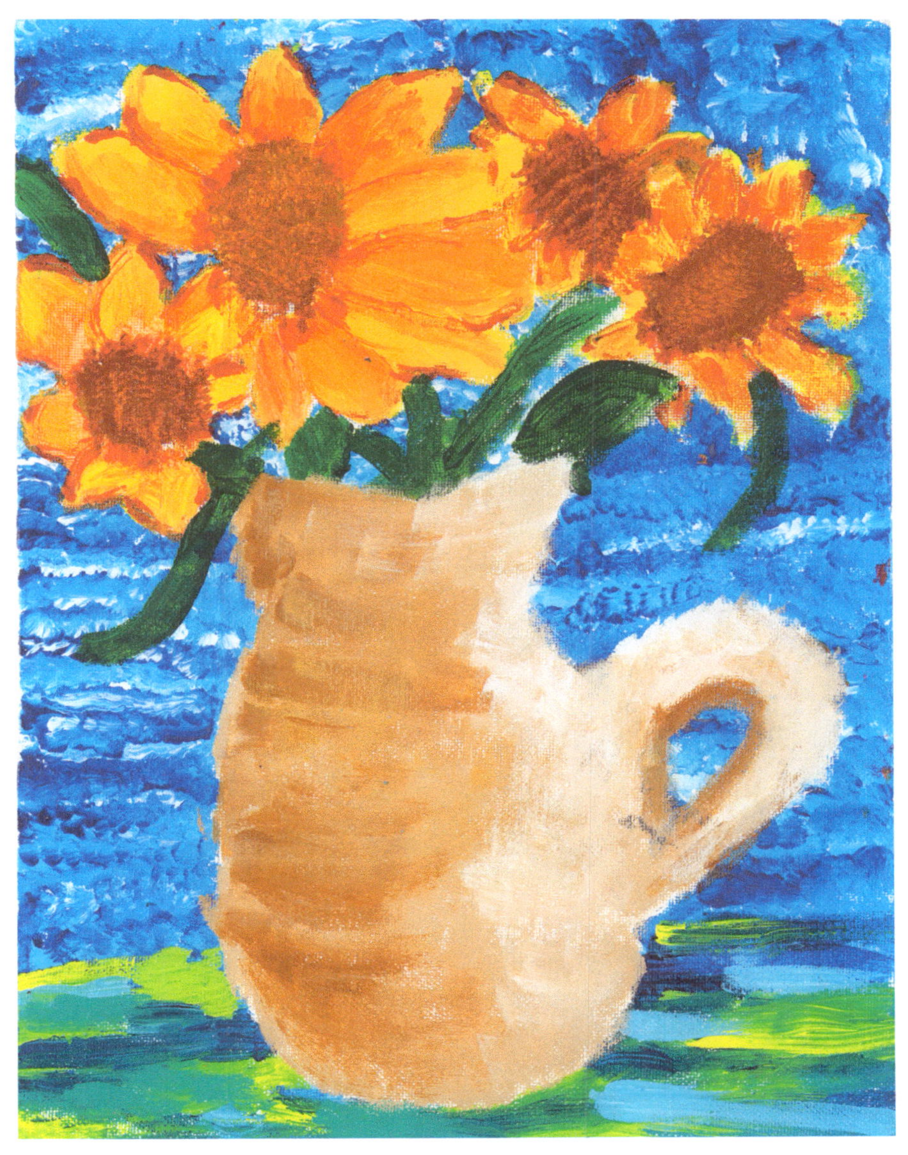

Flowers in Pitcher
Acrylic on canvas, 12 x 9 inches
2016

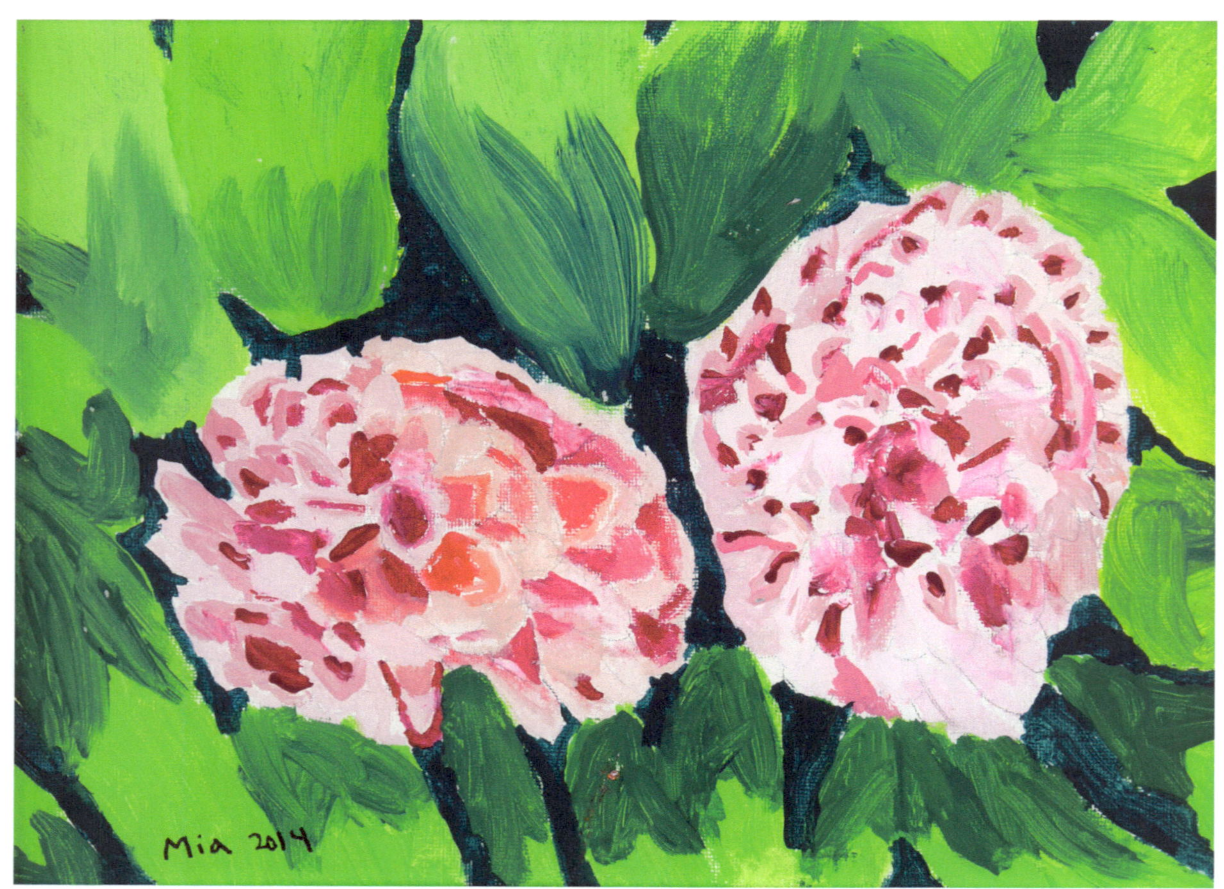

Pink Hydrangea
Acrylic on canvas, 9 x 12 inches
2014

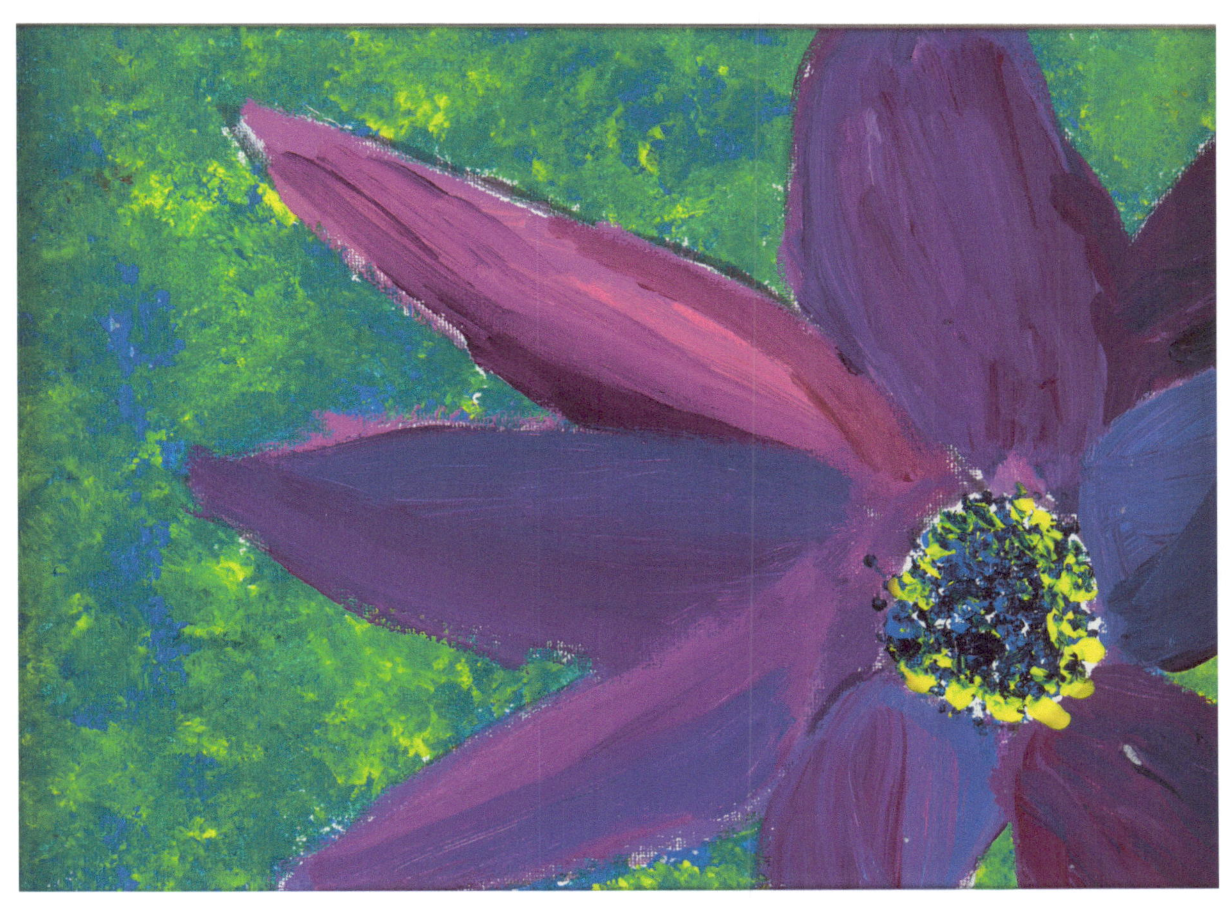

Purple Flower
Acrylic on canvas, 9 x 12 inches
2016

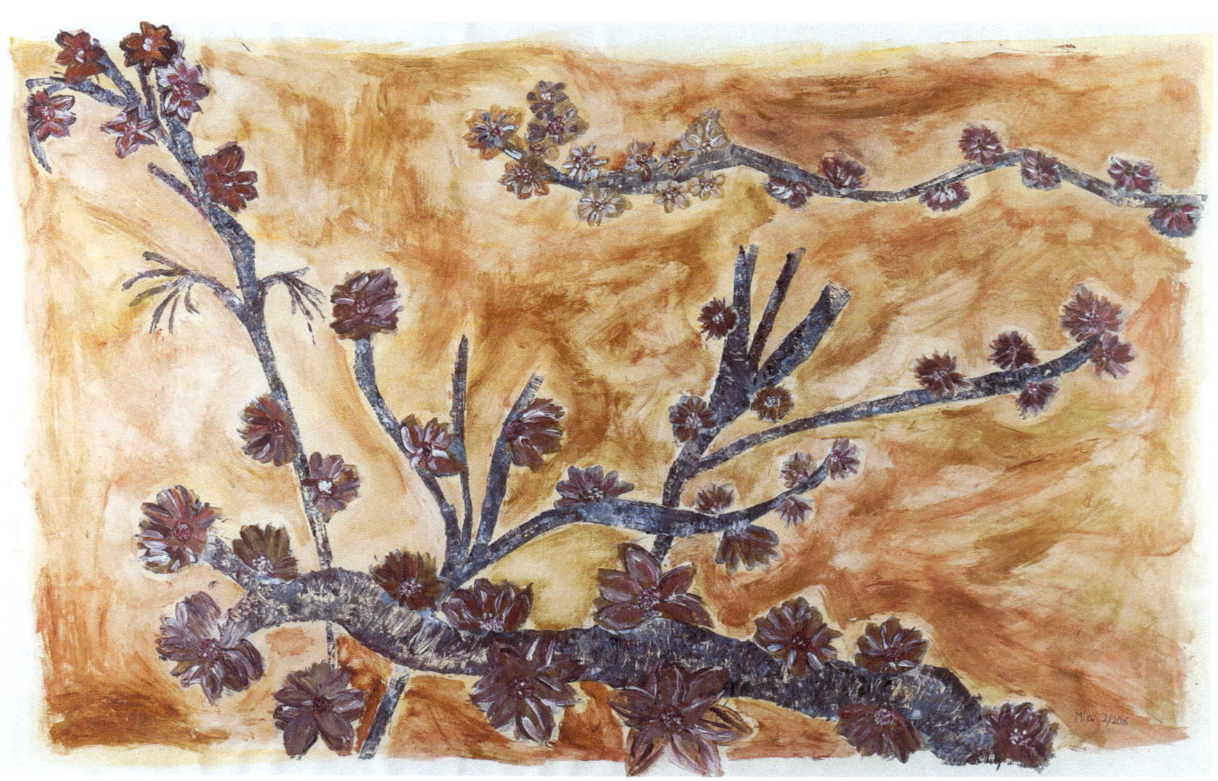

Bamboo Flowers
Acrylic on paper, 36 x 56 inches
2016

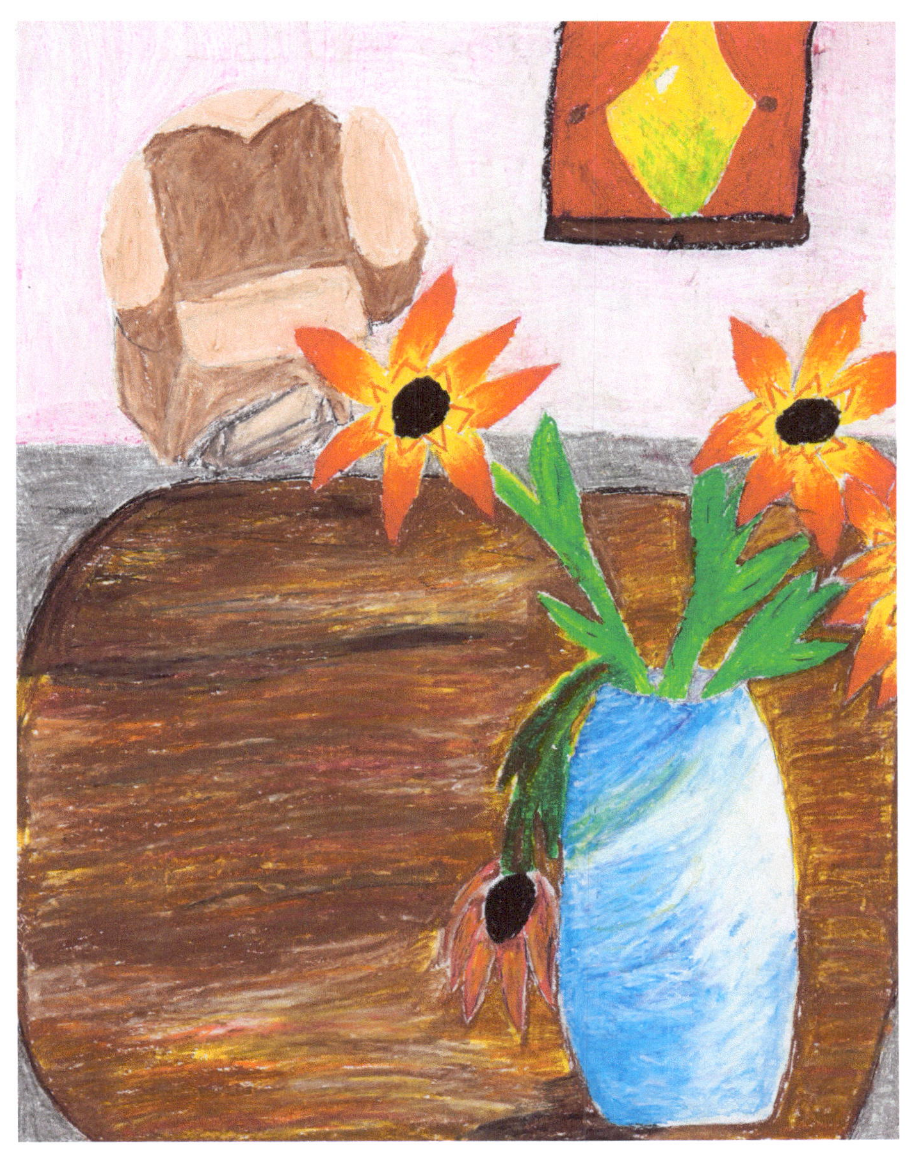

The Living Room
Oil pastel, 26 x 20 inches
2017

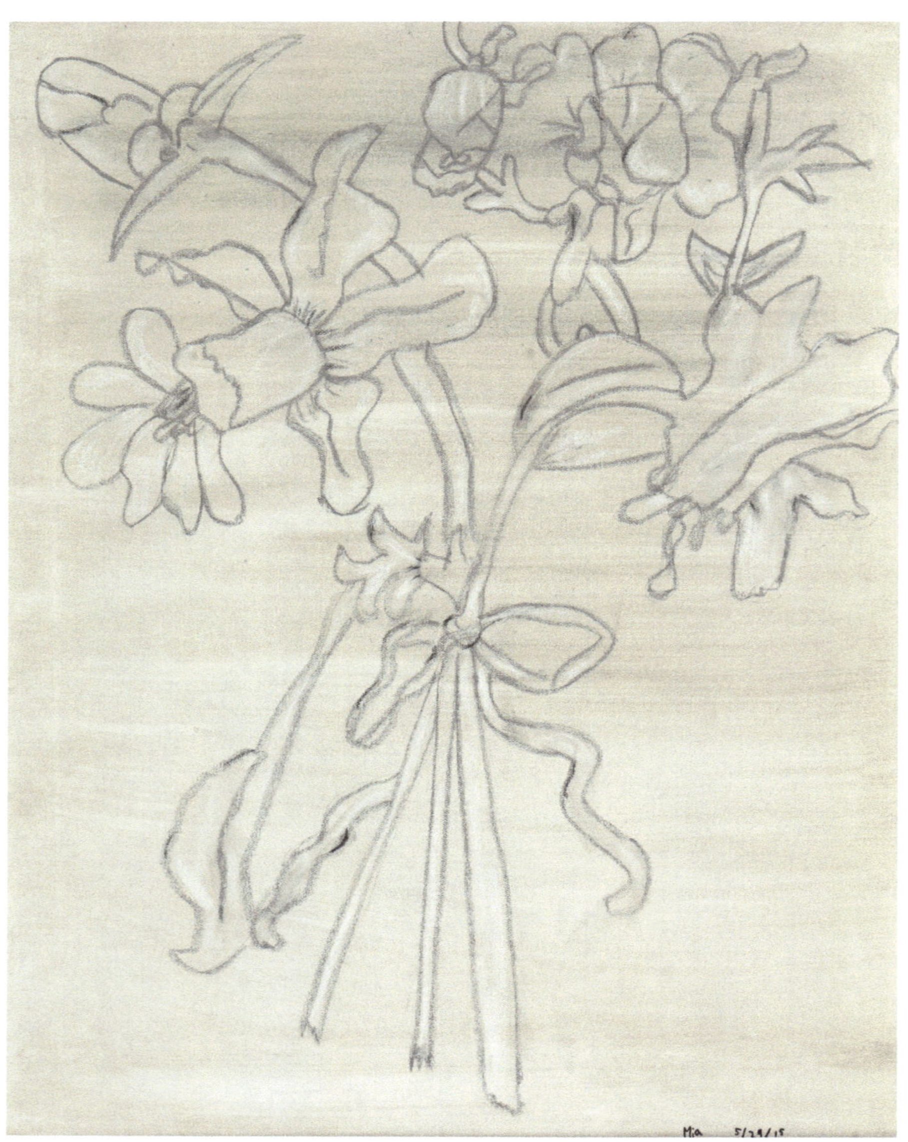

Tied Together
Charcoal, chalk, and acrylic on canvas, 28 x 22 inches
2015

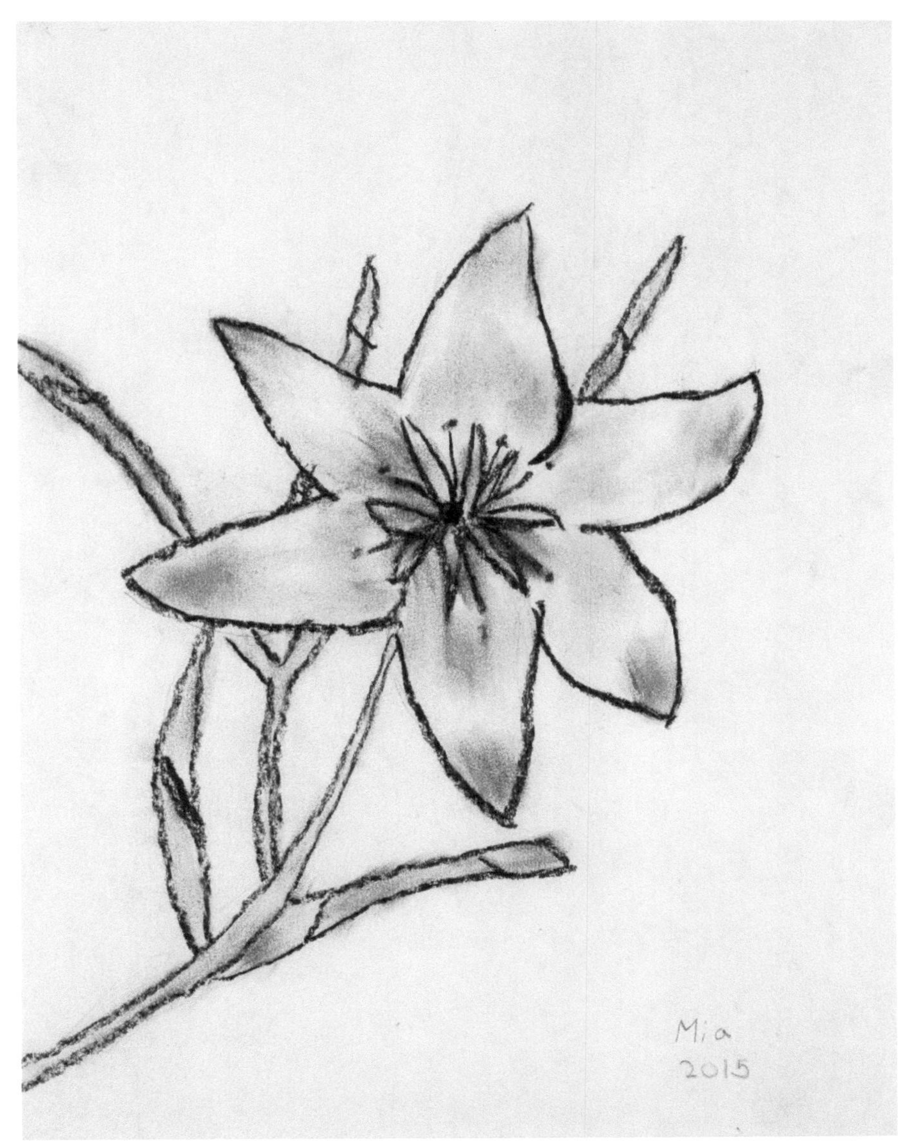

The Charcoal Flower
Charcoal on paper, 12 x 9 inches
2015

Ballerinas

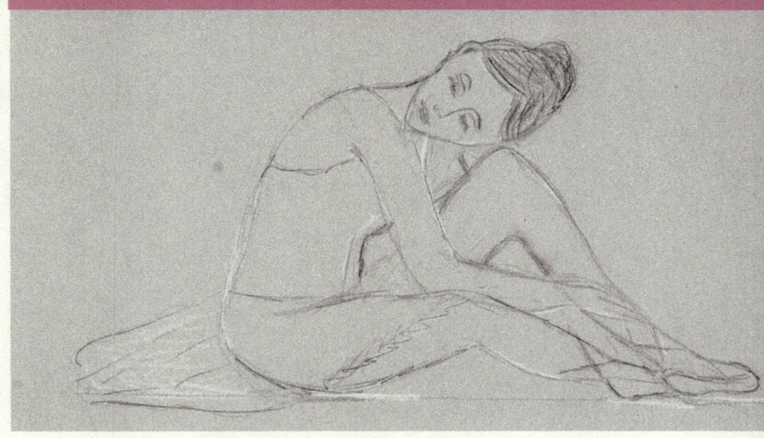

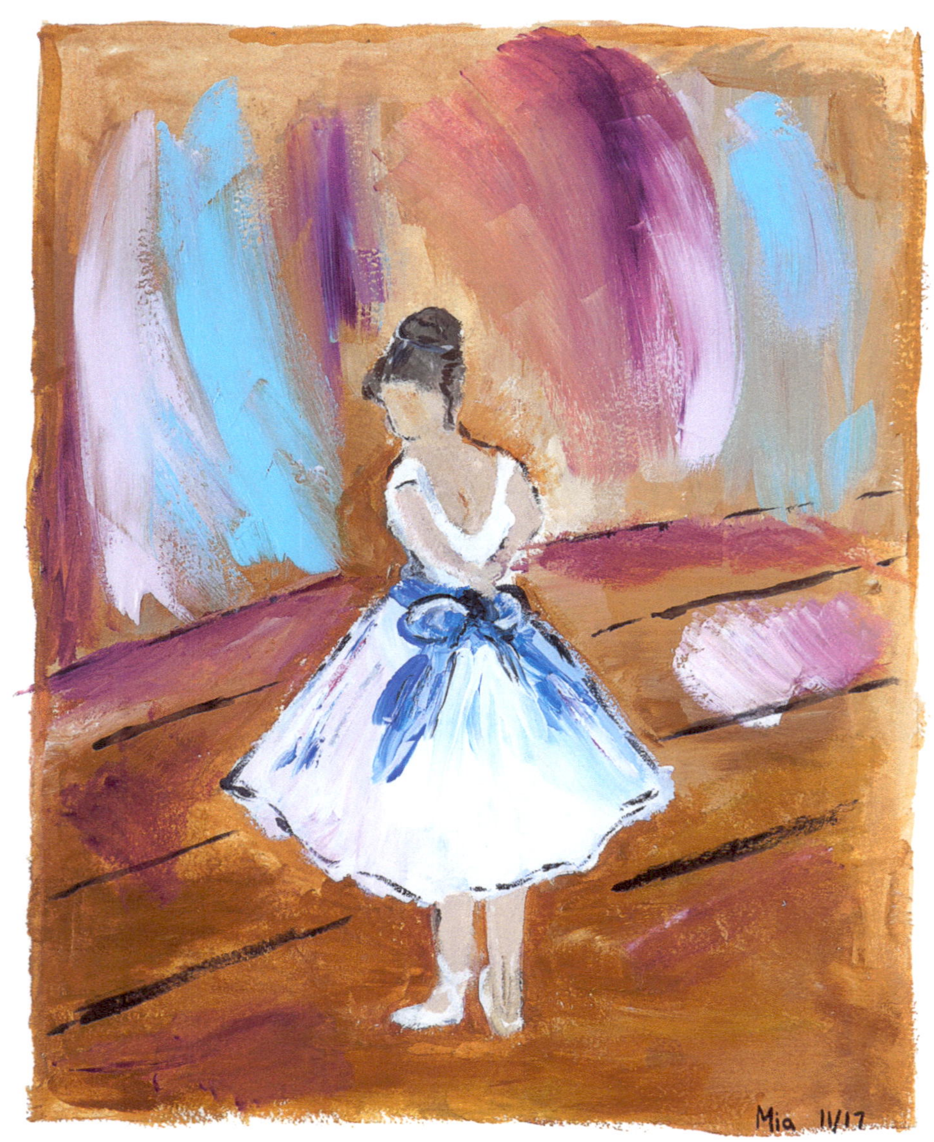

On Stage
Acrylic on paper, 13.5 x 10.5 inches
2017

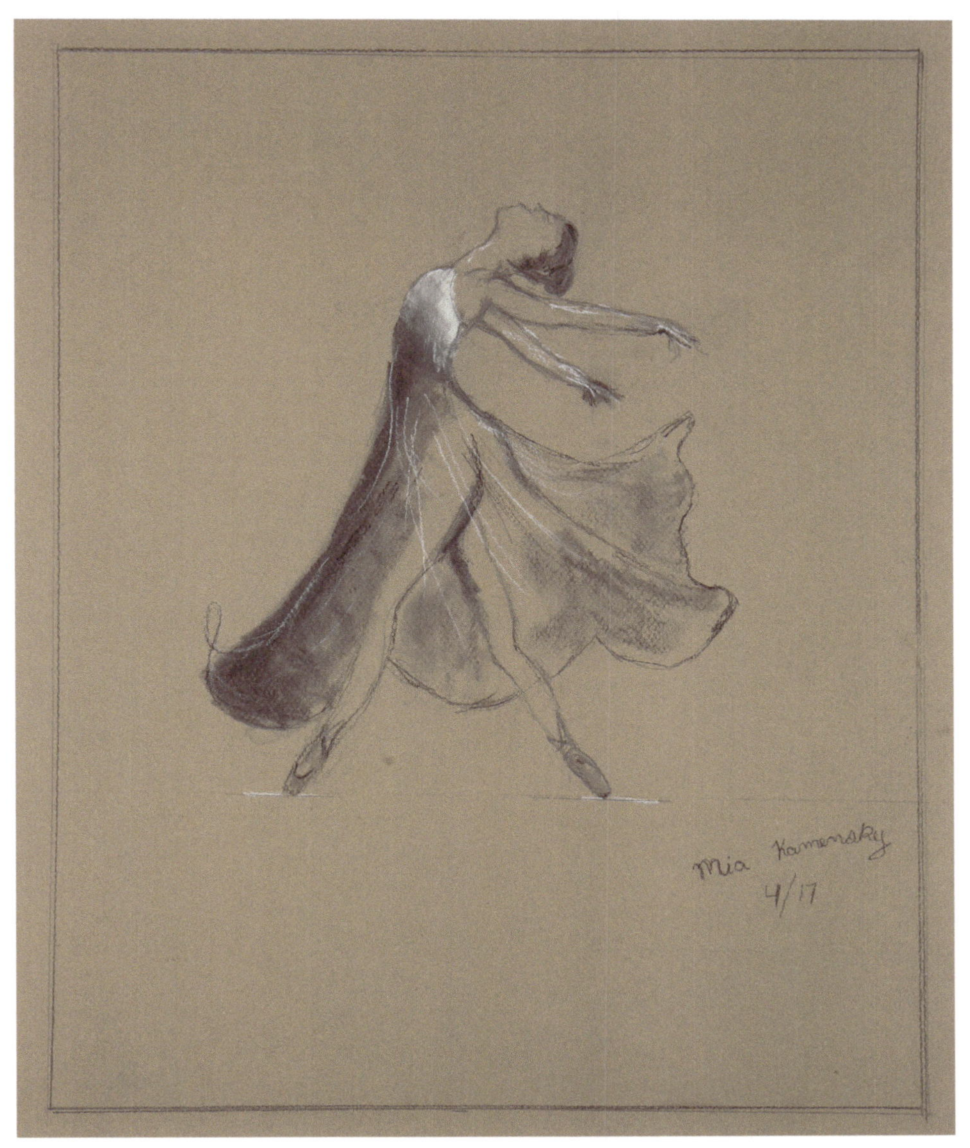

Dancer I
Charcoal and chalk on paper, 25.5 x 20 inches
2017

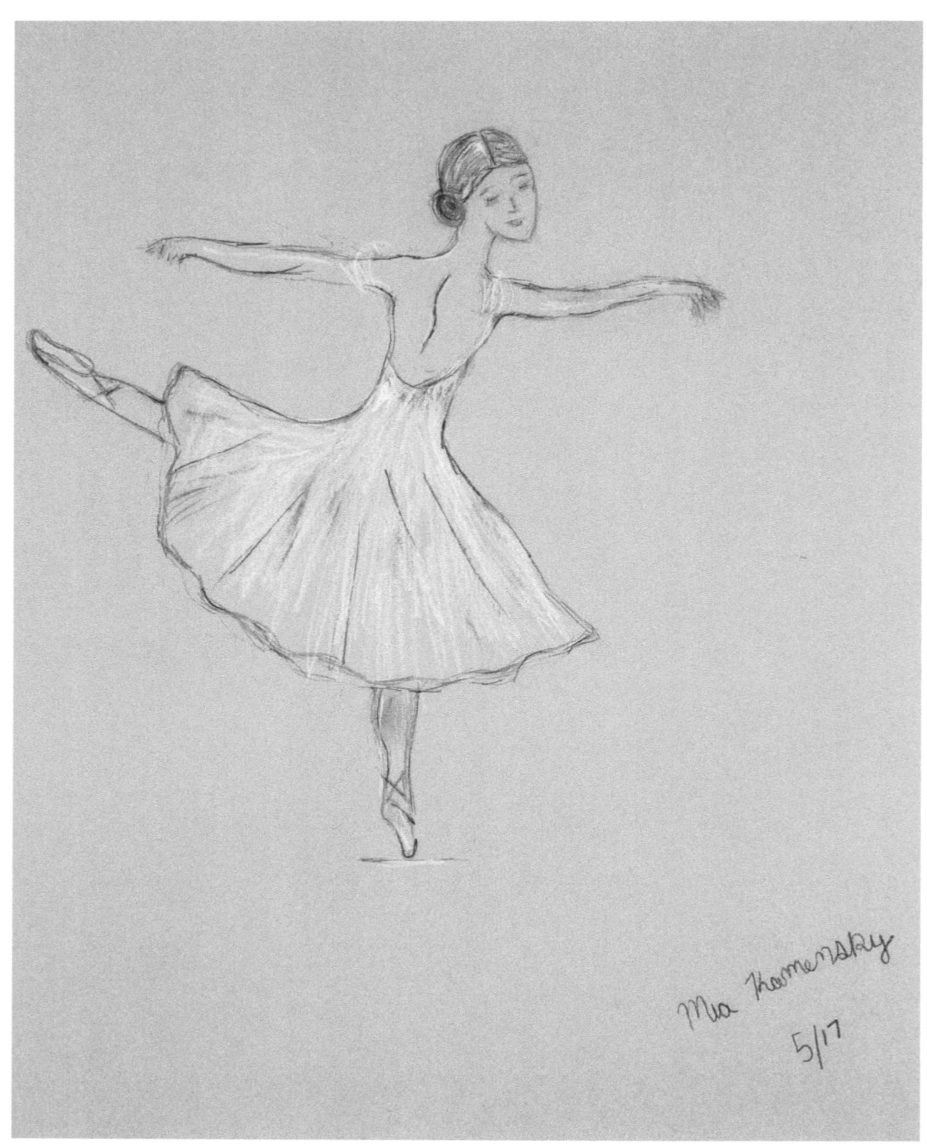

Dancer II
Charcoal and chalk on paper, 24 x 19 inches
2017

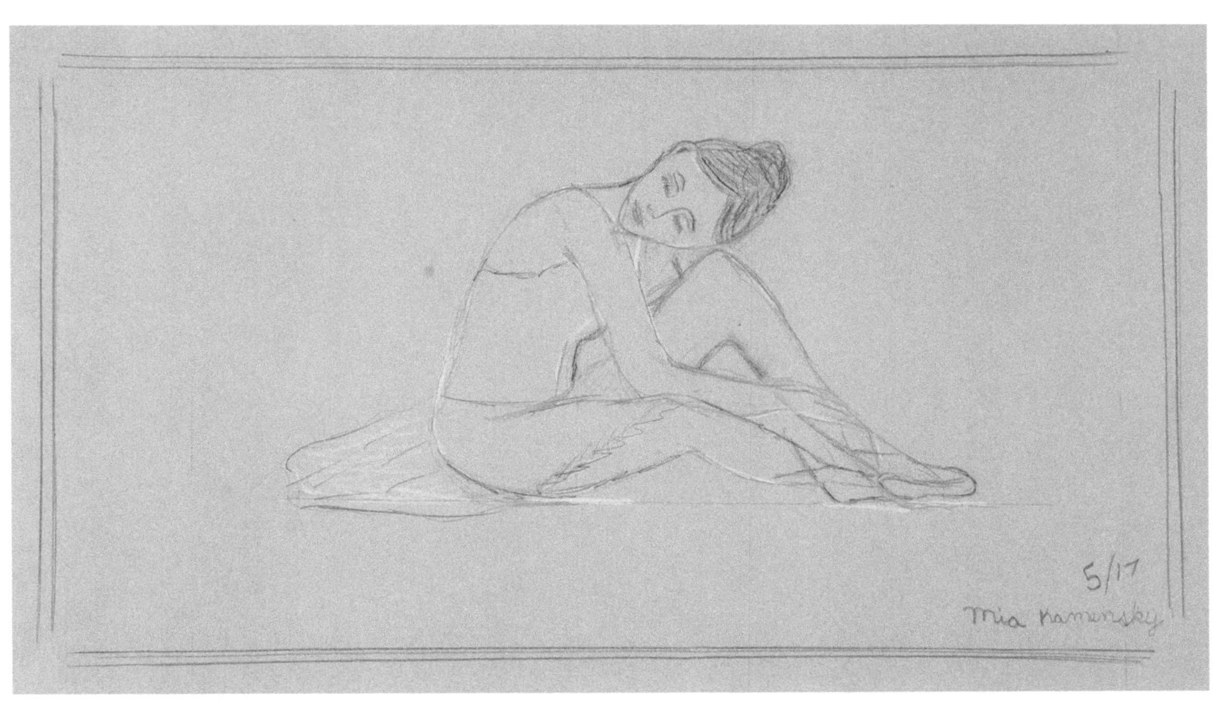

Dancer III
Charcoal and chalk on paper, 12 x 19 inches
2017

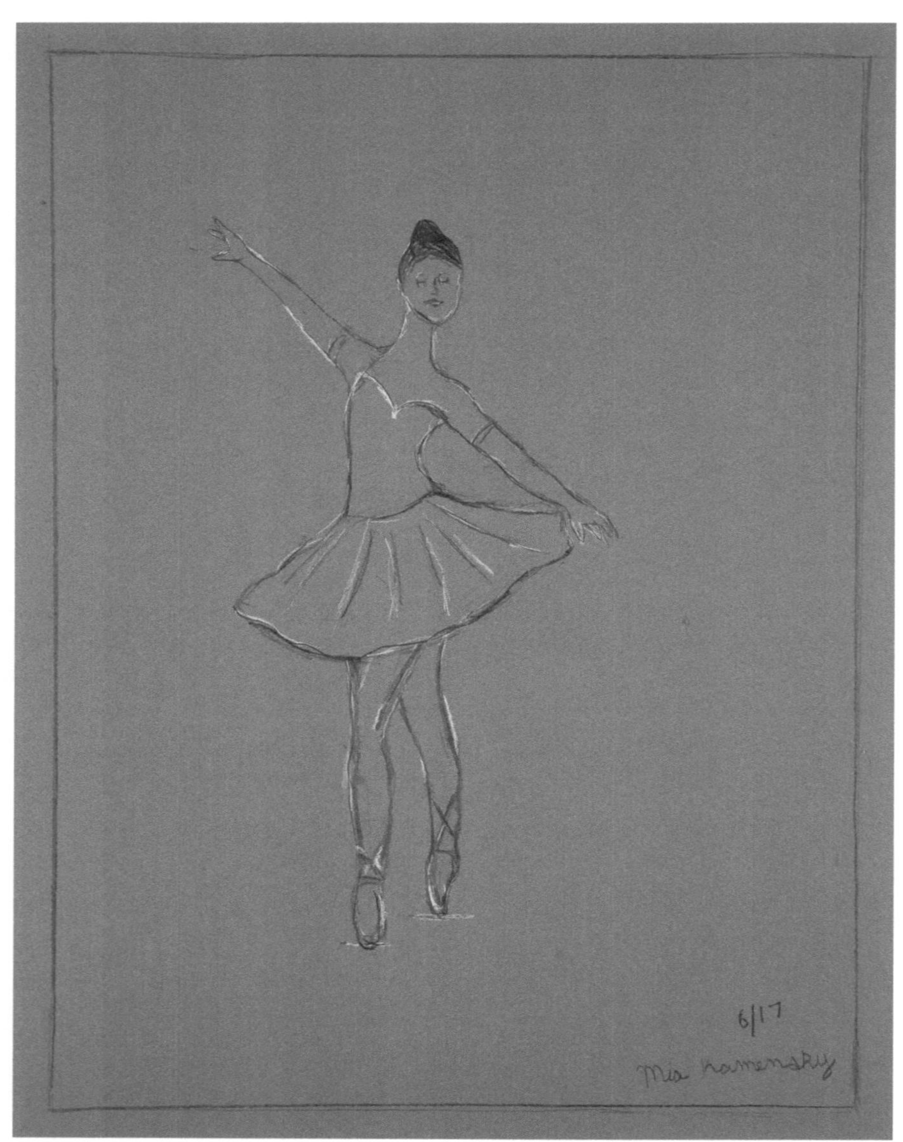

Dancer IV
Charcoal and chalk on paper, 16 x 12 inches
2017

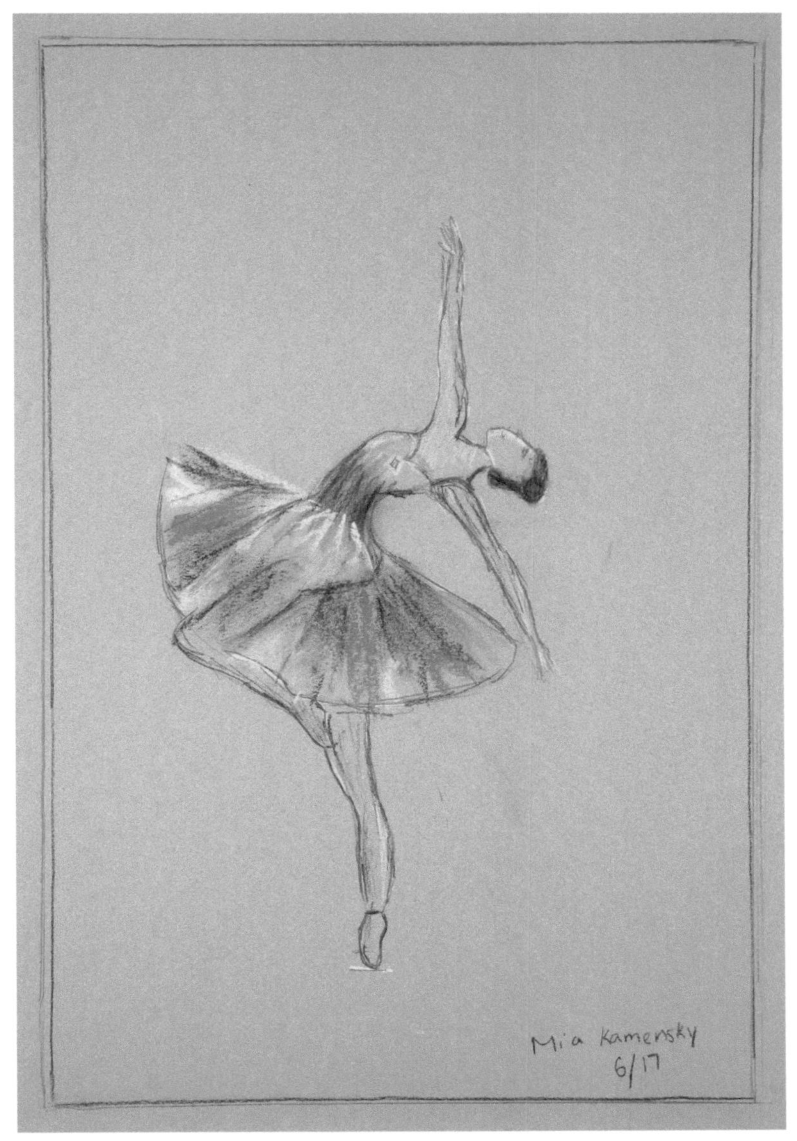

Dancer V
Charcoal and chalk on paper, 19 x 15 inches
2017

People

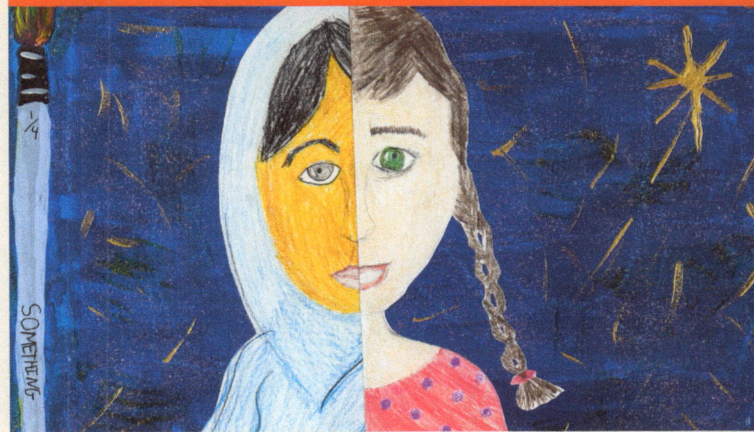

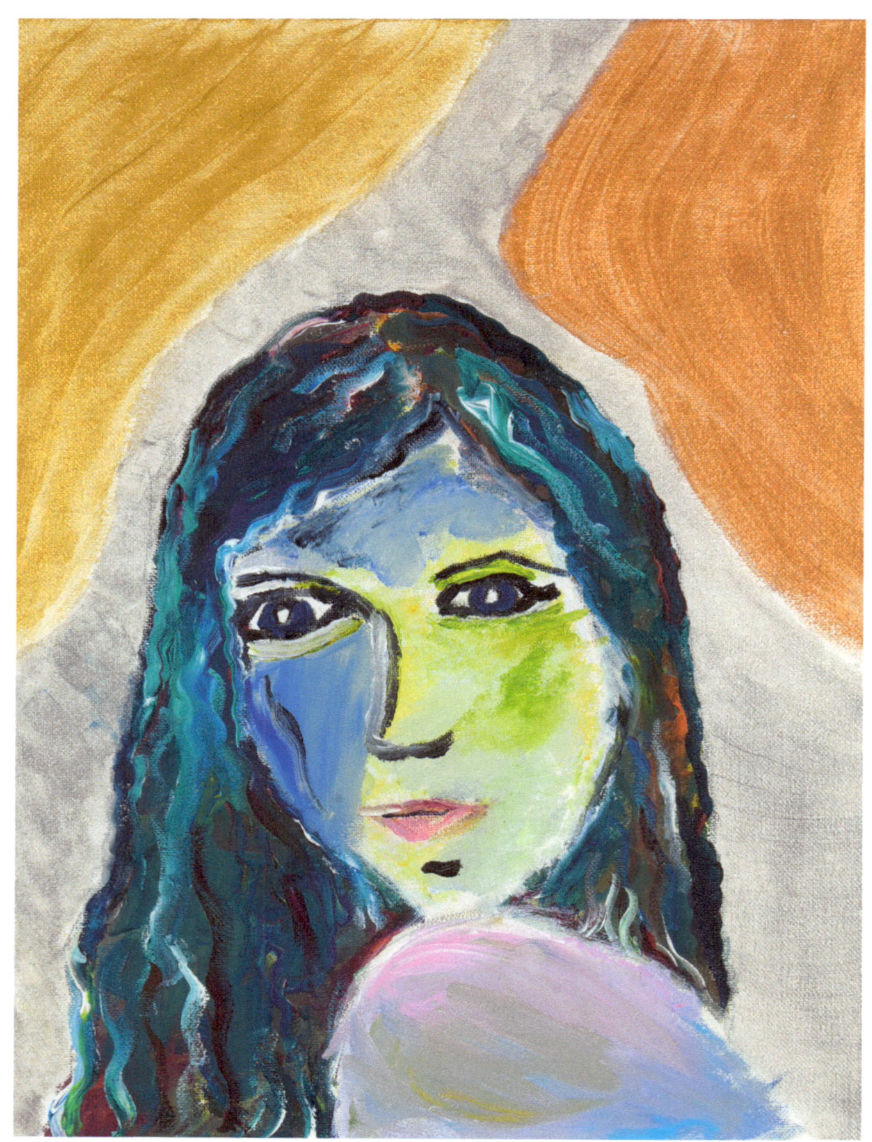

Long Haired Girl
Acrylic on canvas, 16 x 12 inches
2016

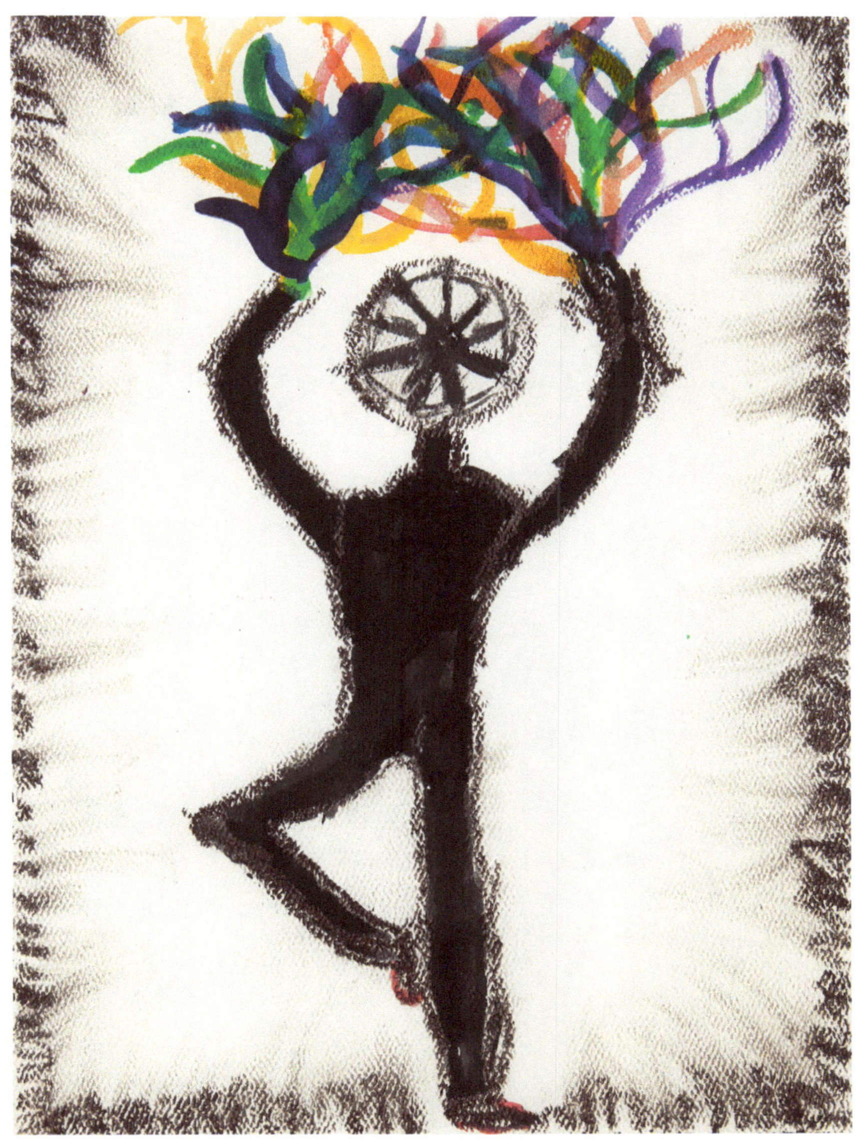

Tree Pose
Oil pastel and watercolor on paper, 12 x 9 inches
2016

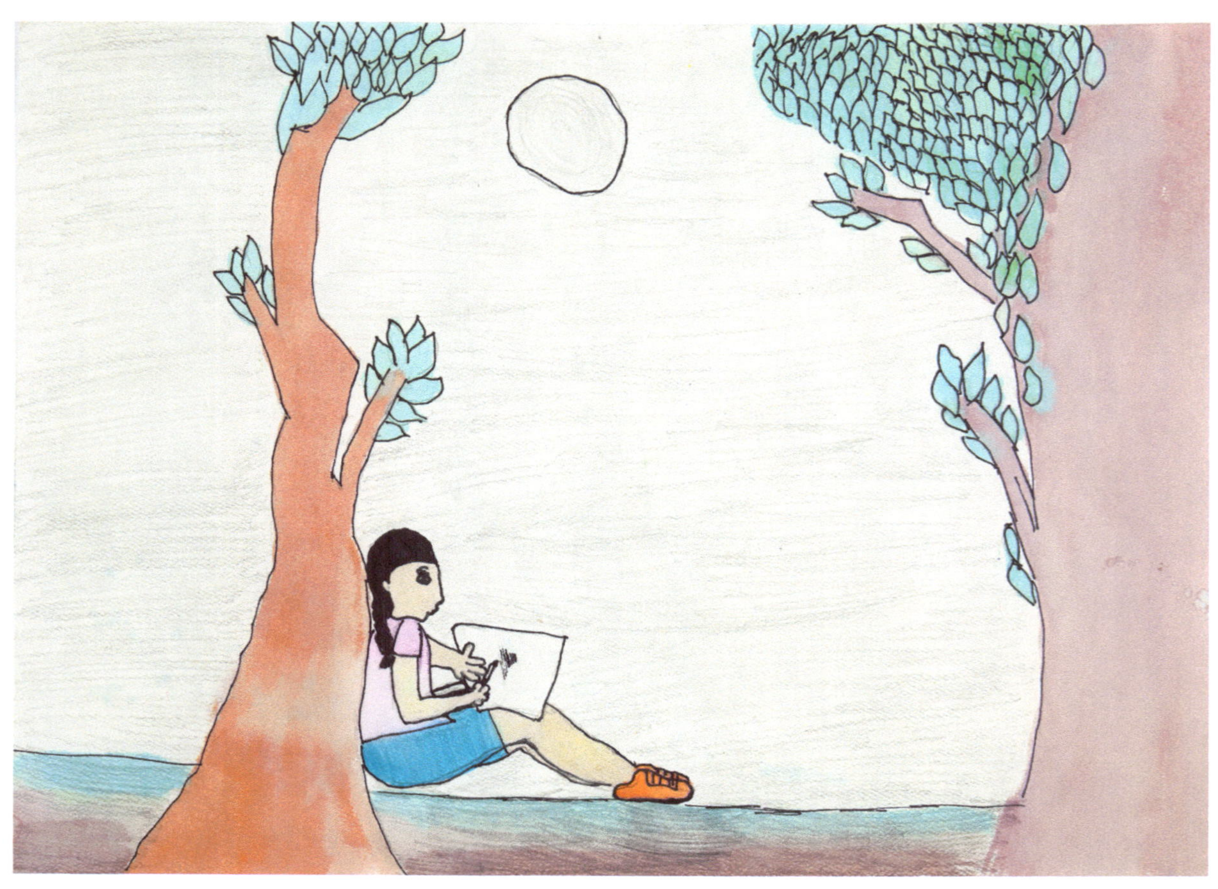

Shading
Ink, graphite, and watercolor on paper, 11 x 15 inches
2017

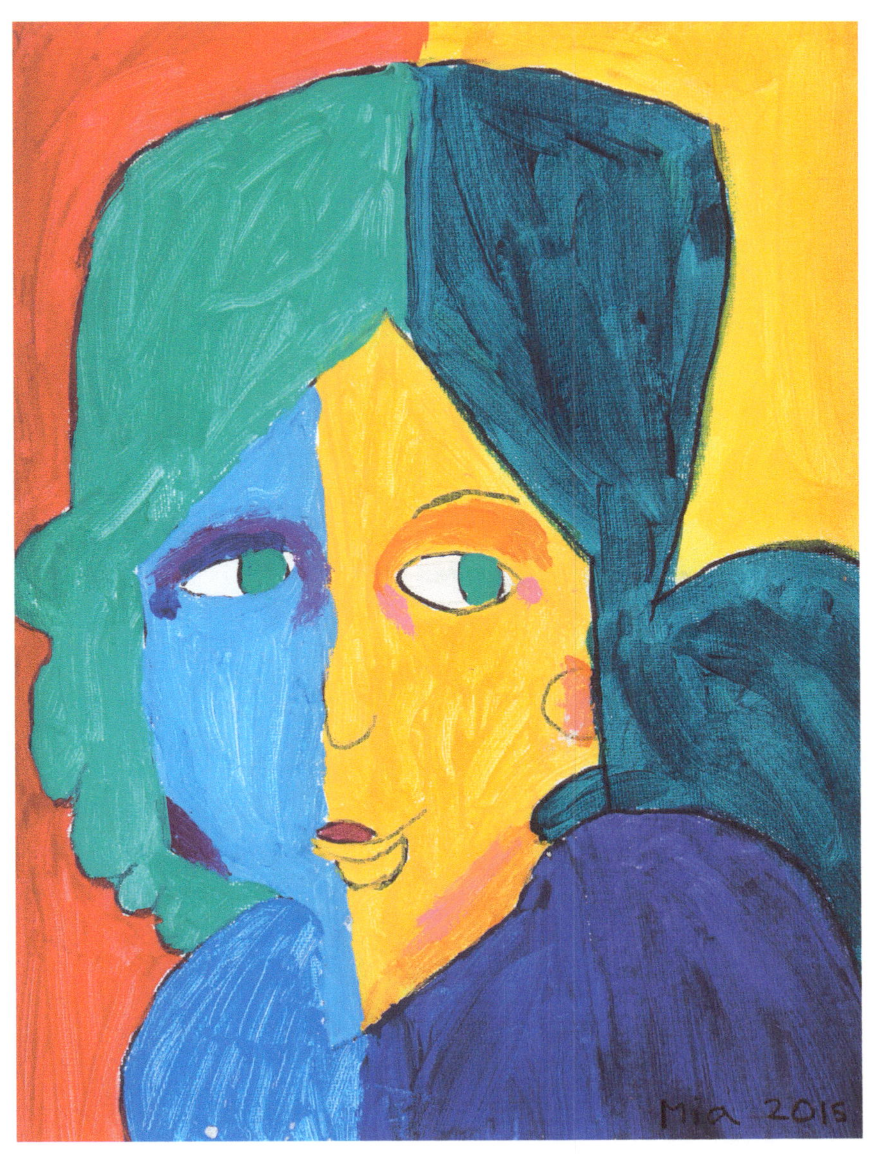

Primary Woman
Acrylic on canvas, 12 x 9 inches
2015

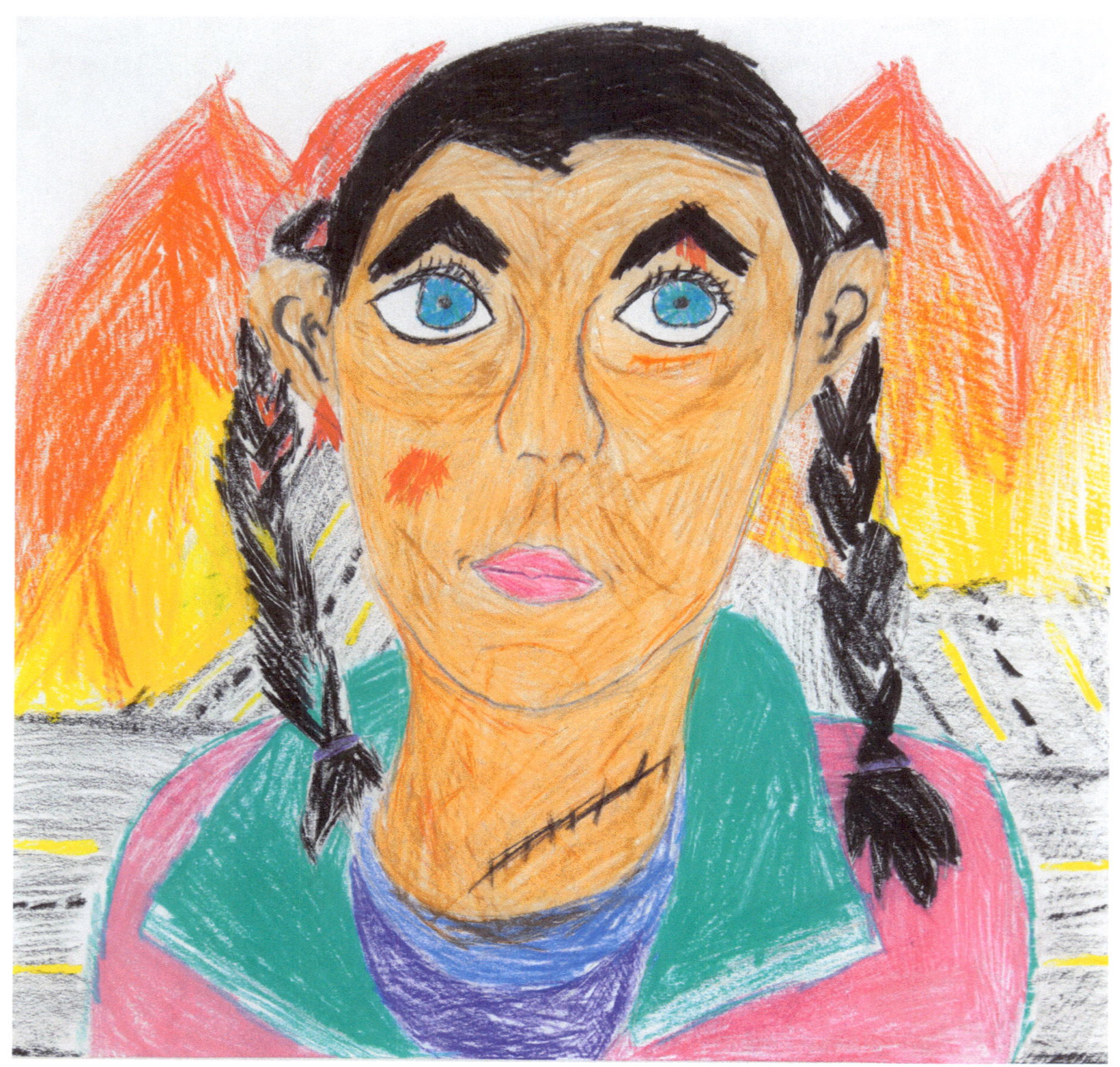

After the Fire
Colored pencil on paper, 12 x 11.5 inches
2017

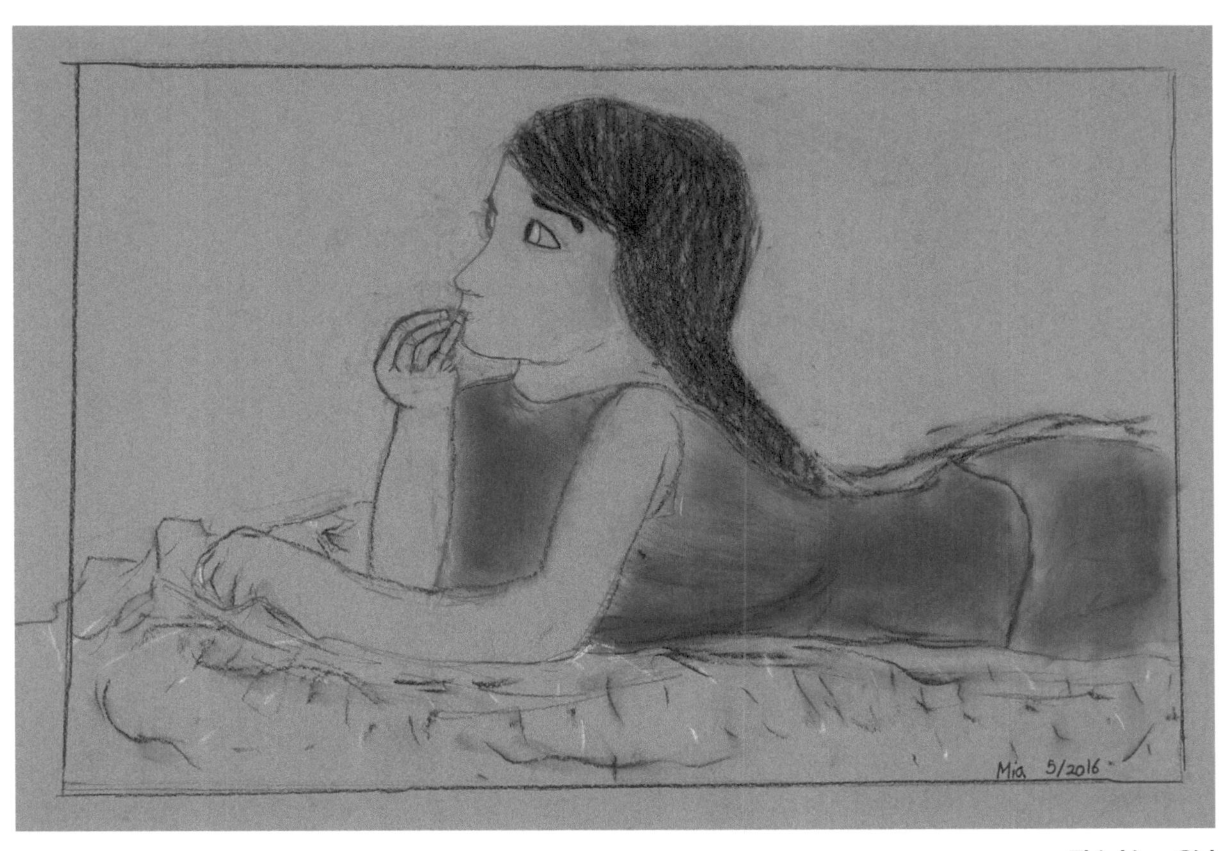

Thinking Girl
Charcoal on paper, 19 x 25 inches
2016

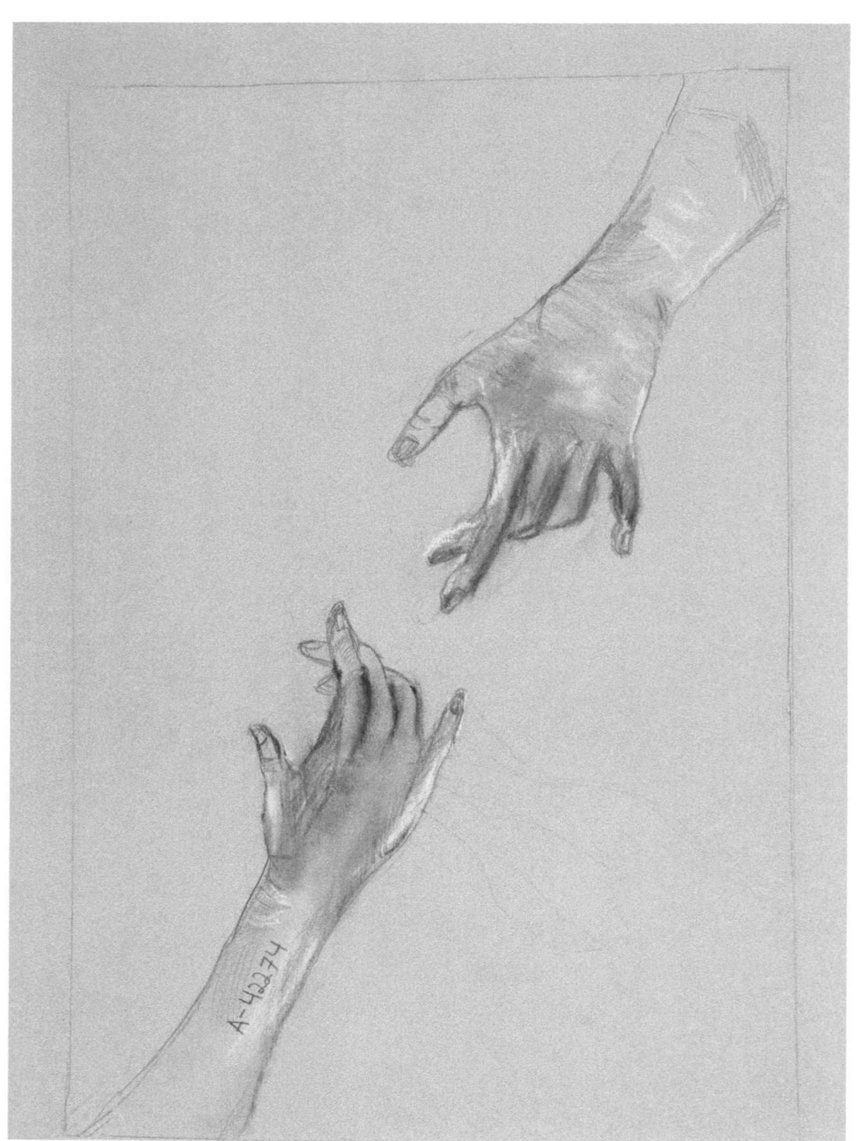

The Space Between Us
Charcoal on paper, 23 x 20 inches
2017

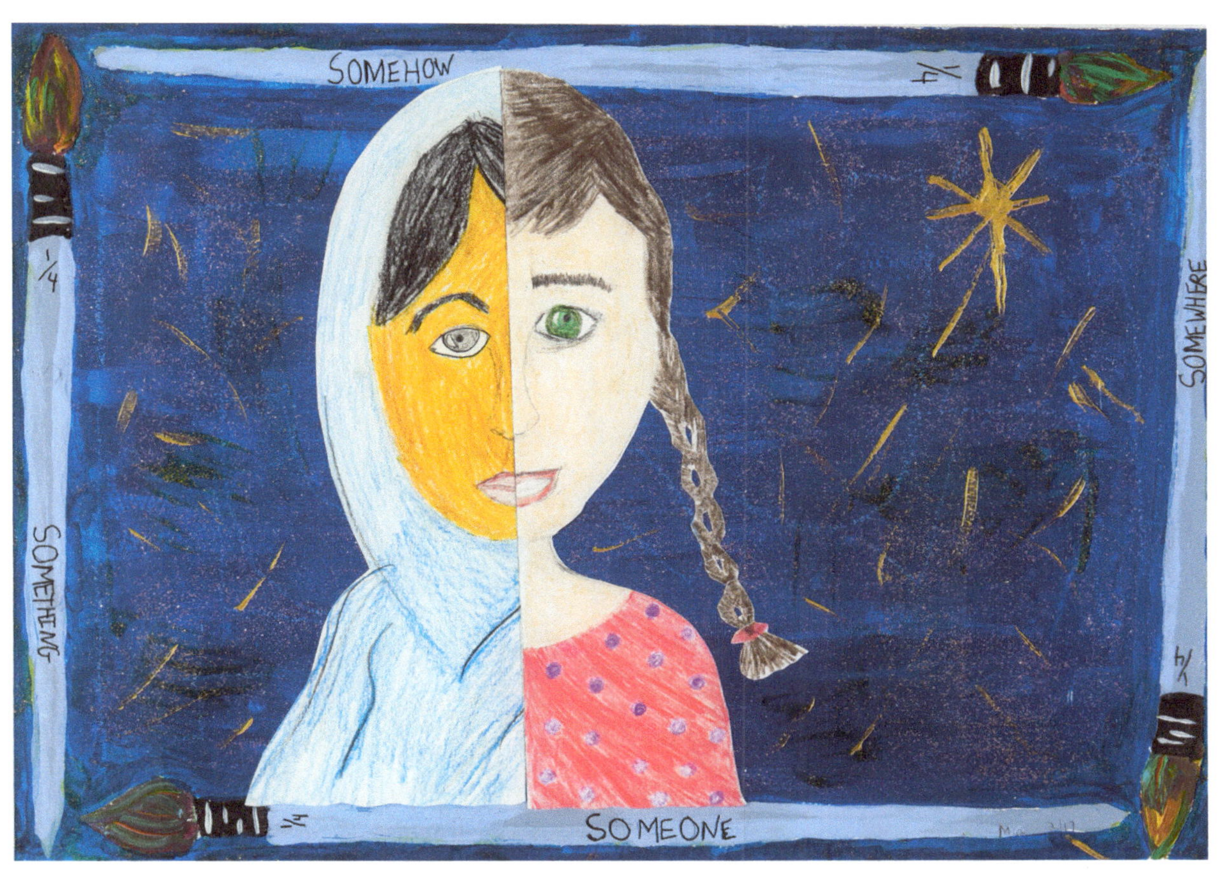

Under One Sky
Colored pencil, acrylic, and glitter on paper, 12 x 16 inches
2017

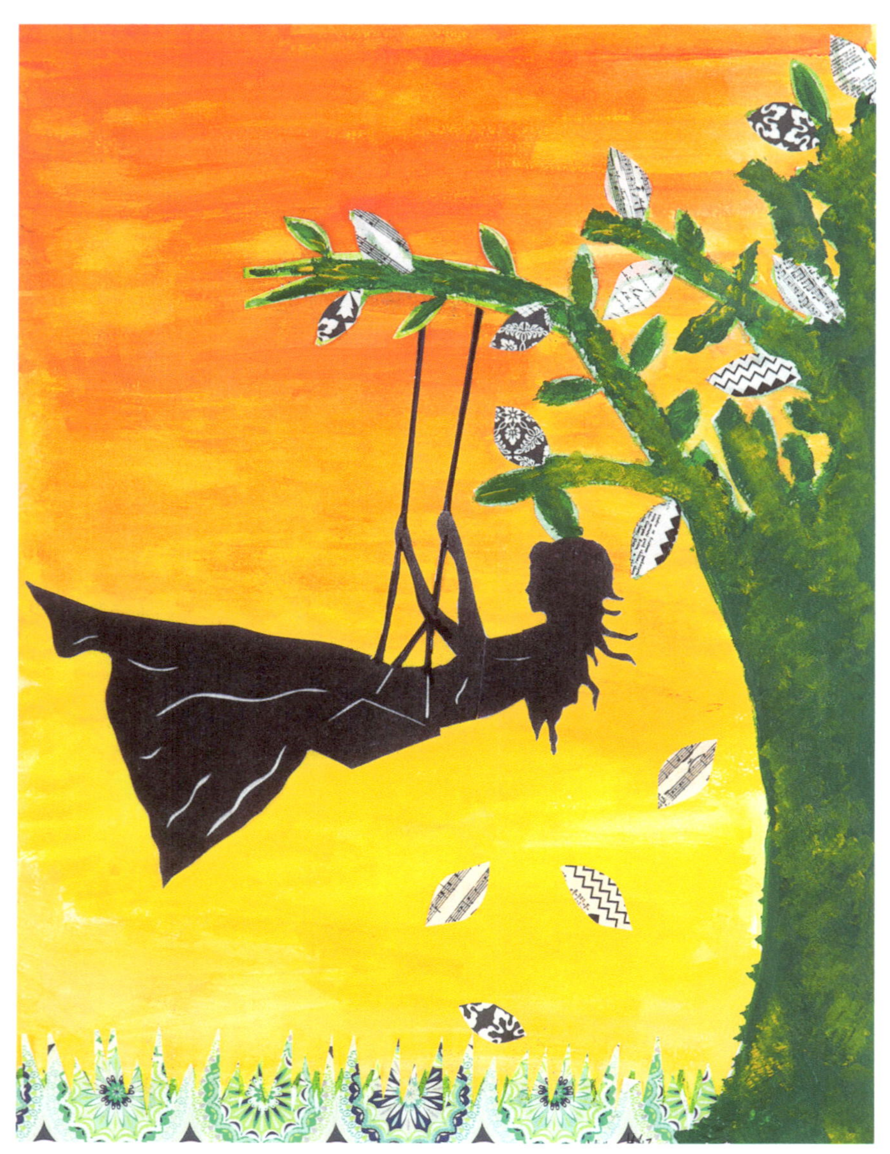

Girl on a Swing
Acrylic, paper, felt collage on paper, 21 x 15.75 inches
2017

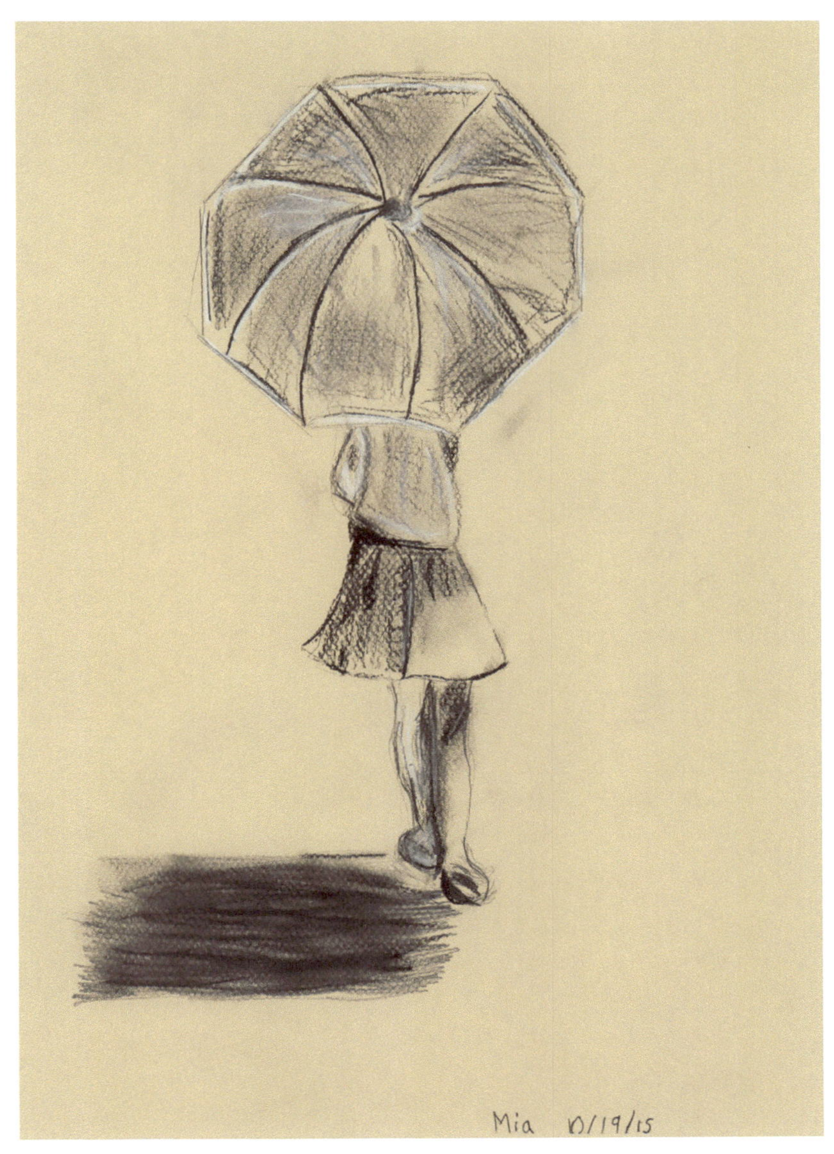

Girl with an Umbrella
Charcoal on paper, 15 x 10.5 inches
2015

Nature

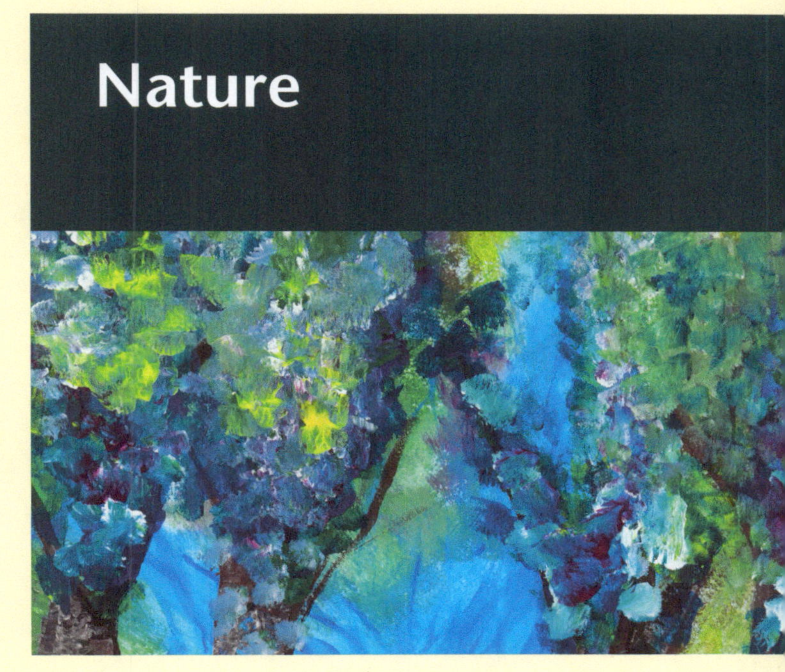

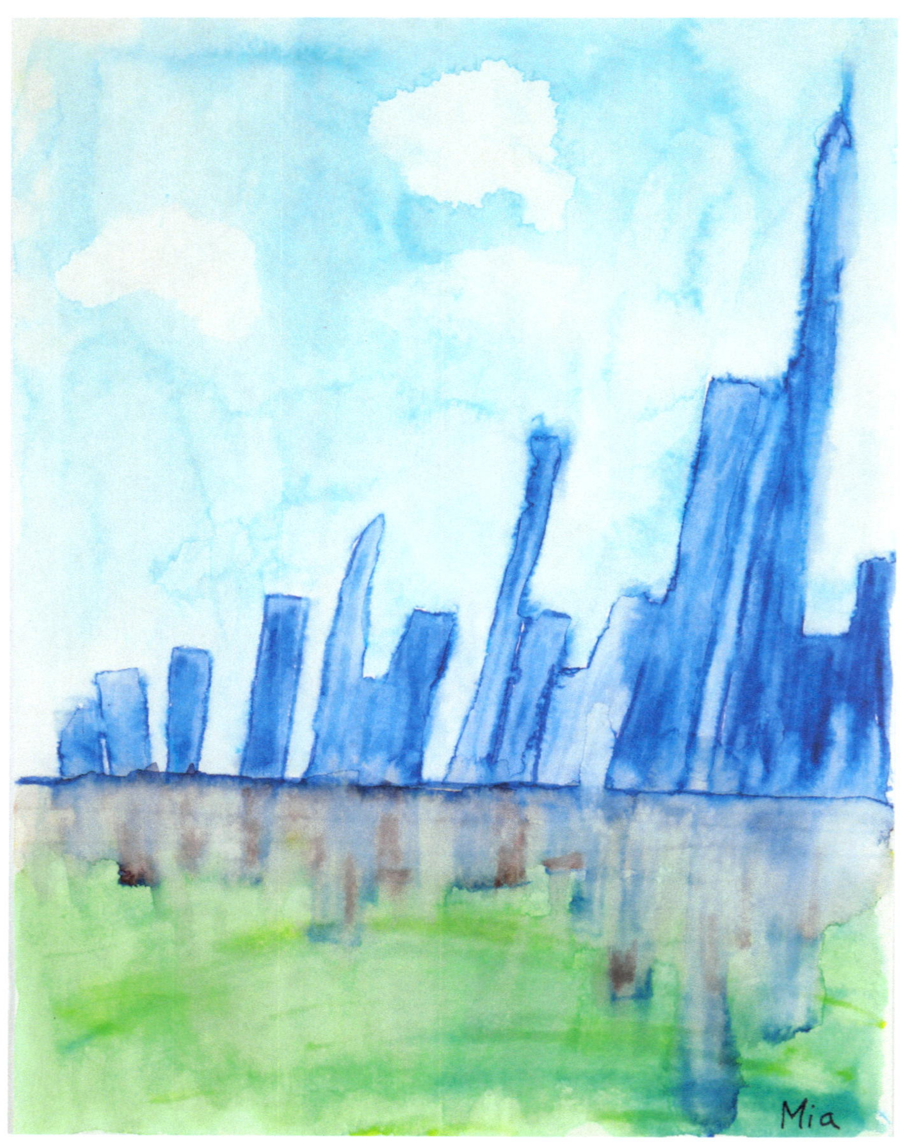

My View
Watercolor on paper, 12 x 9 inches
2014

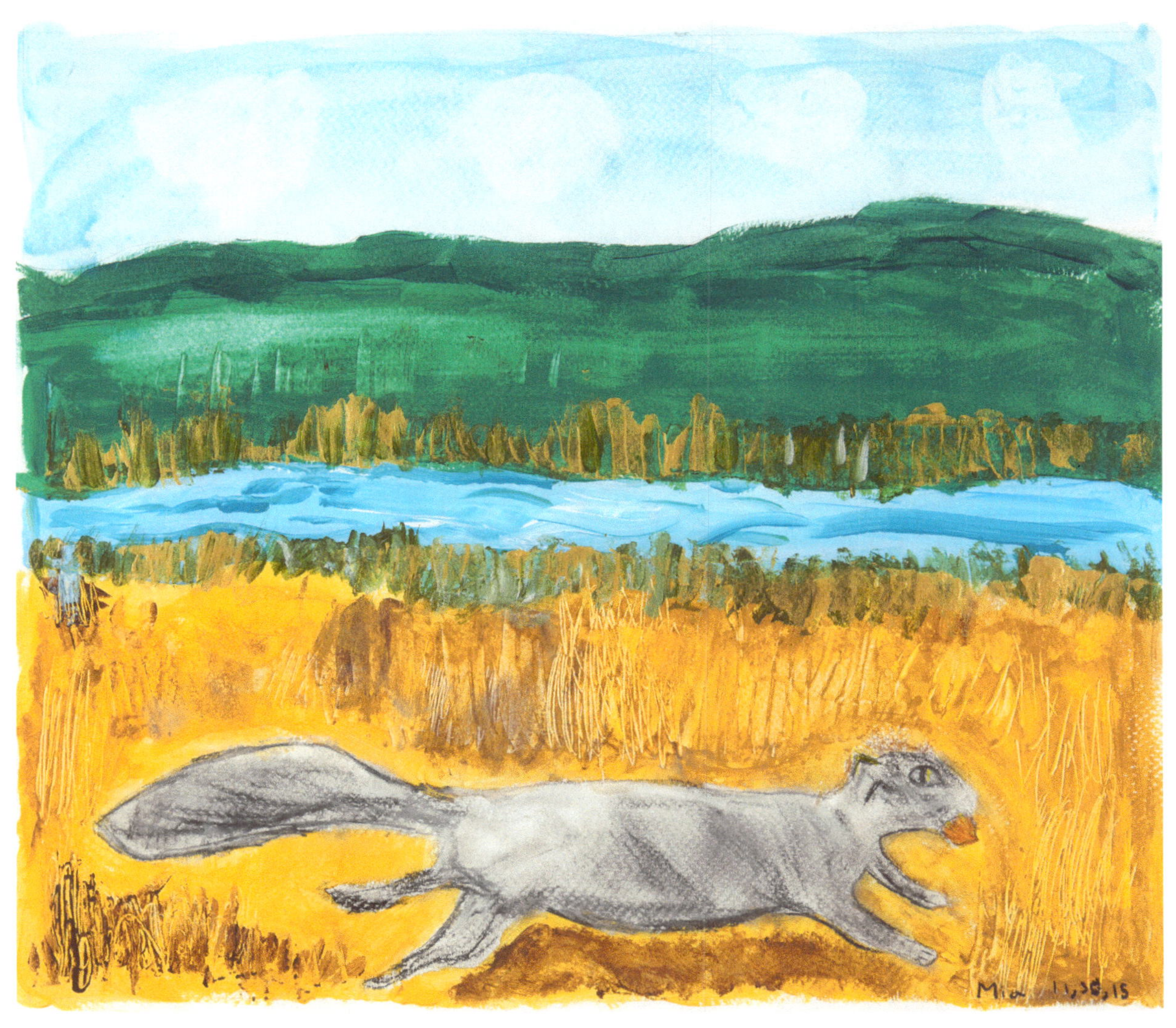

In the Field
Watercolor, acrylic, and charcoal on paper, 11.5 x 13 inches
2015

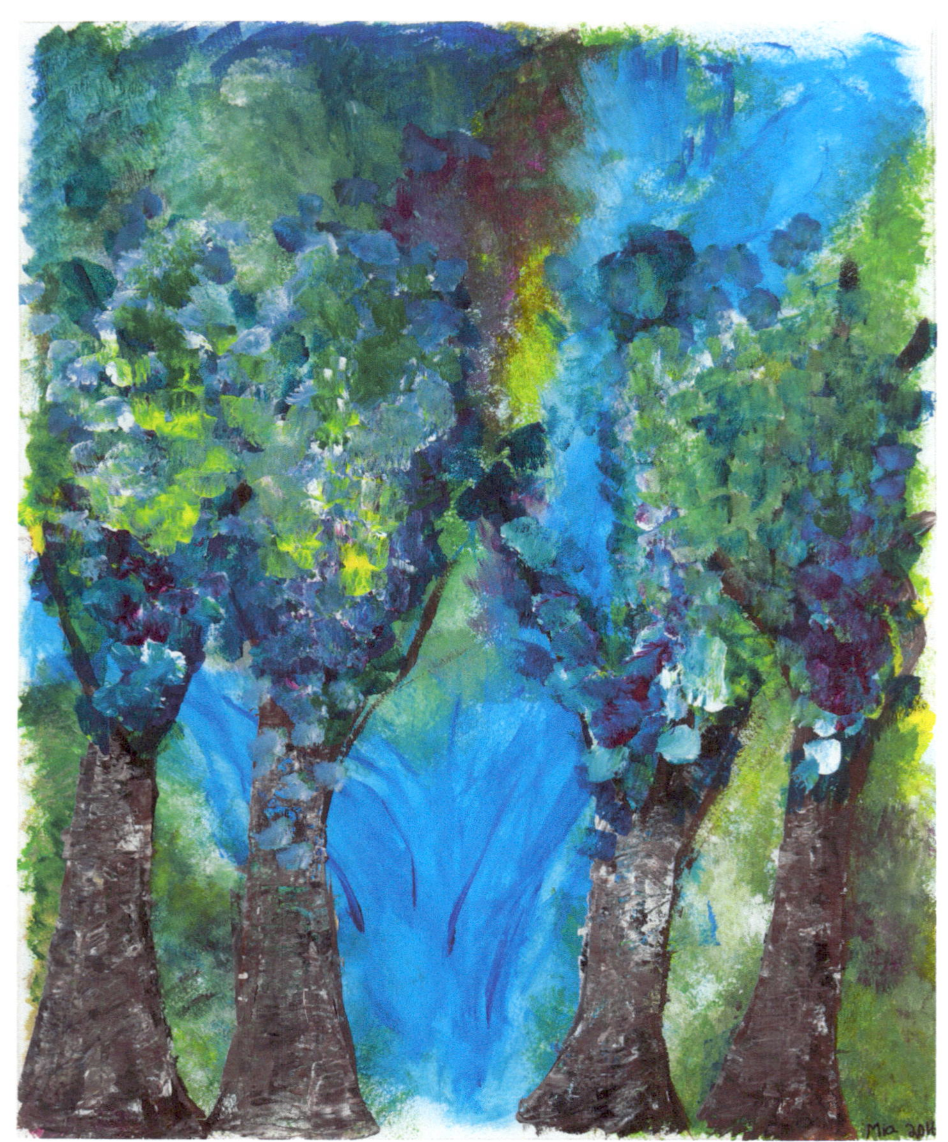

Waterfall
Acrylic on paper, 20 x 16 inches
2016

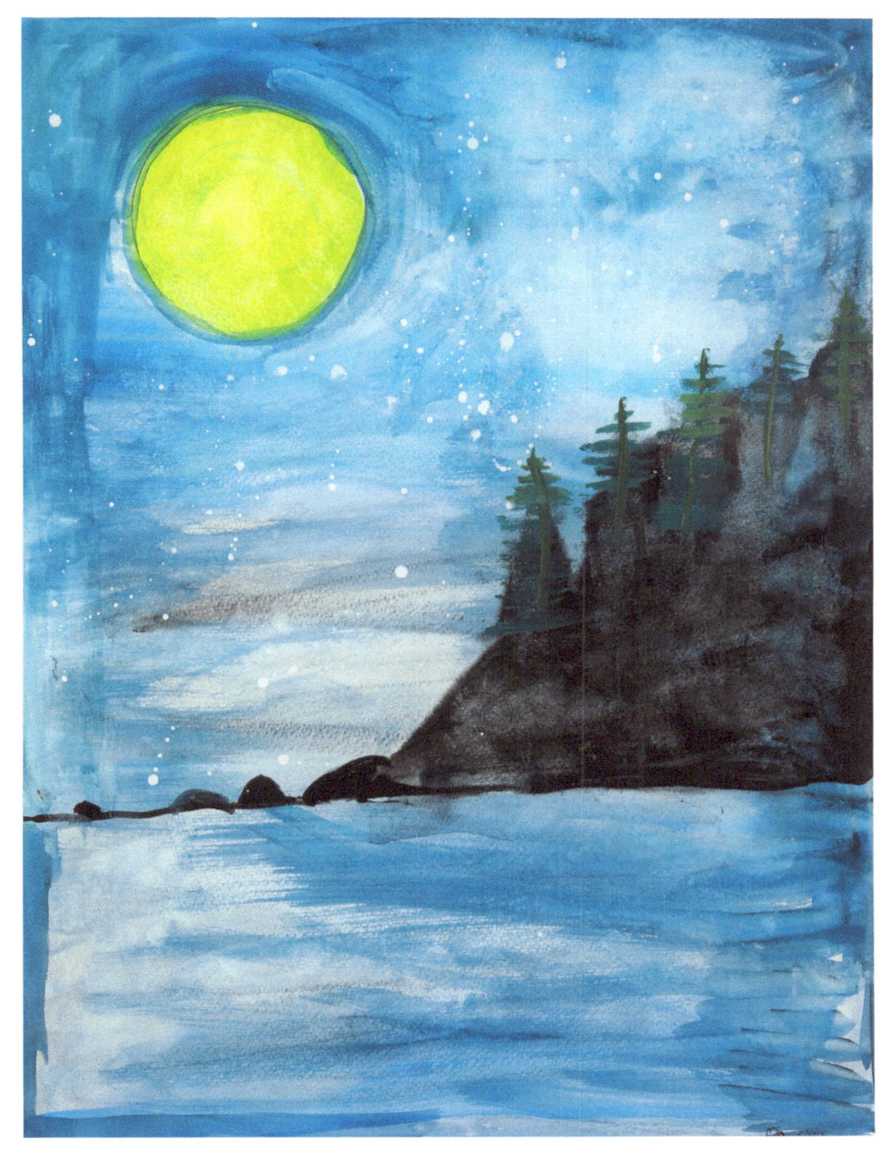

Inspired by Starry Night
Watercolor and acrylic on paper, 23 x 17 inches
2015

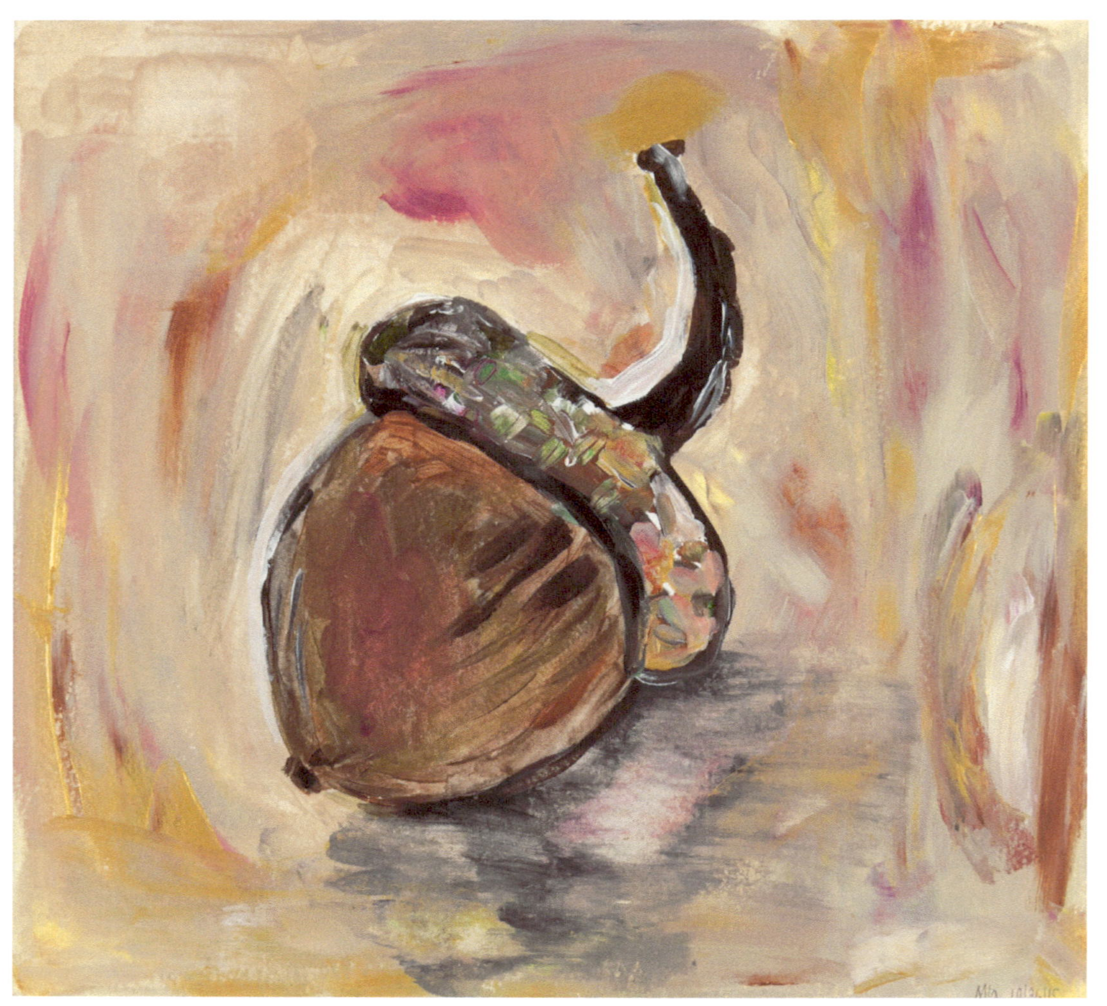

The Acorn
Acrylic on paper, 12.5 x 12 inches
2015

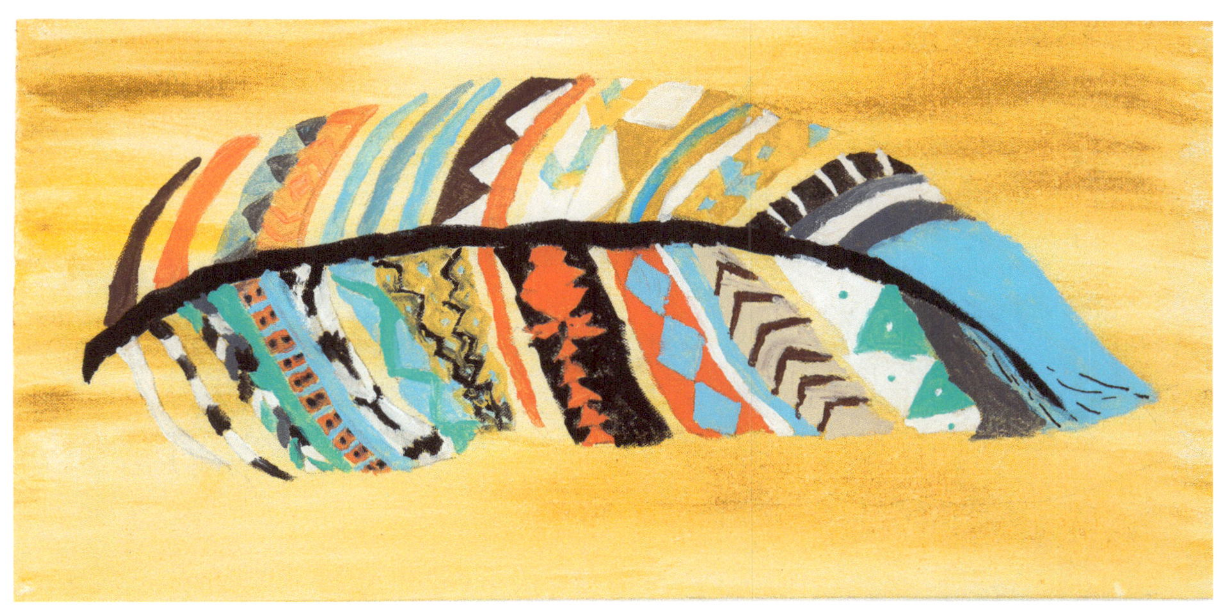

The Feather
Acrylic on canvas, 12 x 24 inches
2014

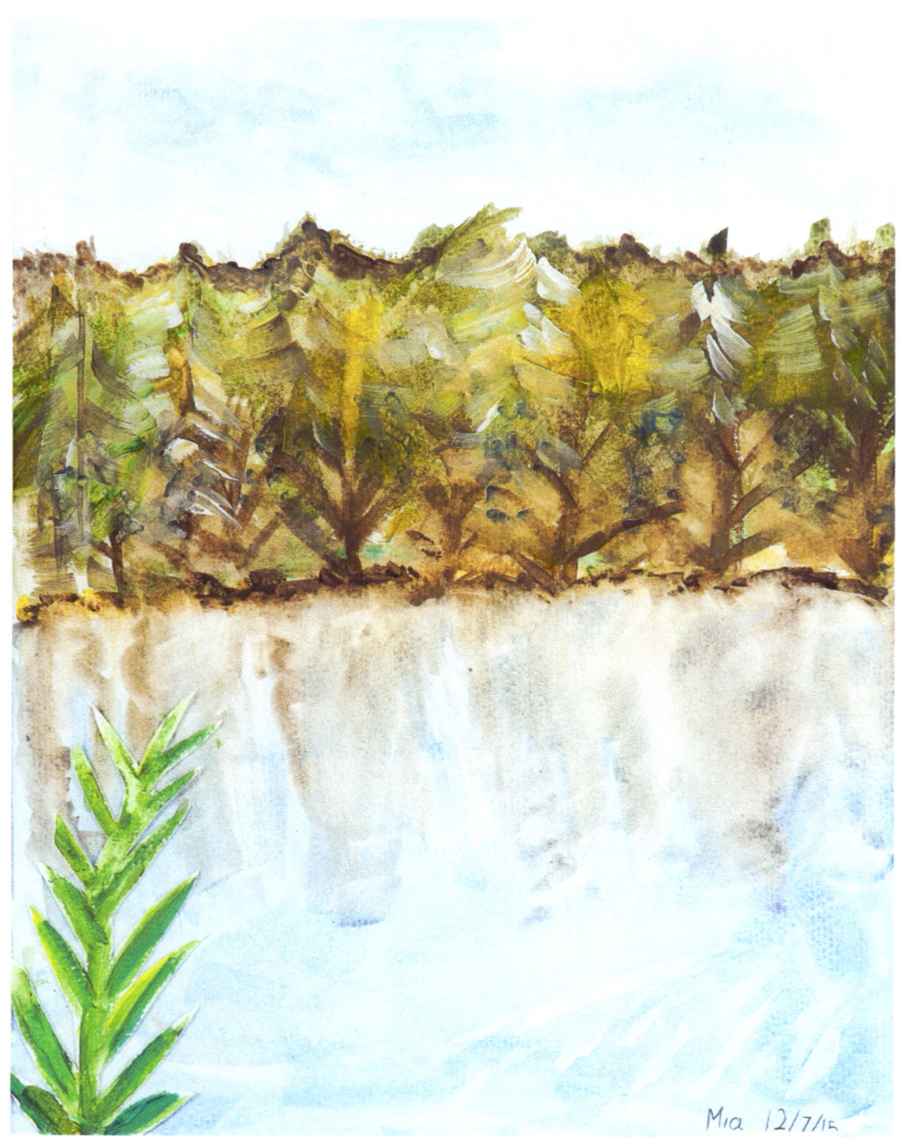

Reflection
Watercolor on paper, 13.5 x 10.5 inches
2015

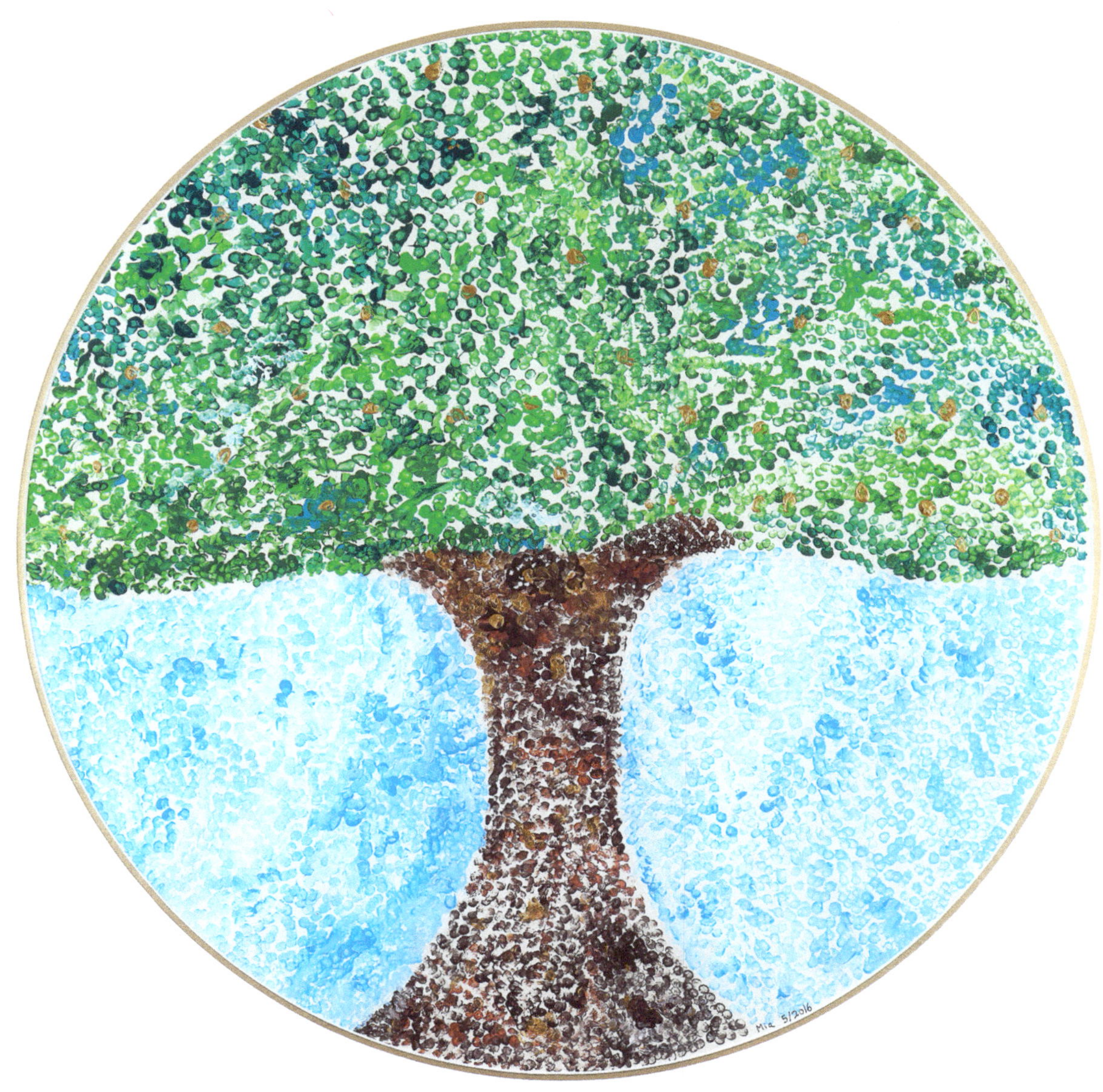

Tree of Life
Acrylic on paper, 28.5 inches diameter
2016

Animals

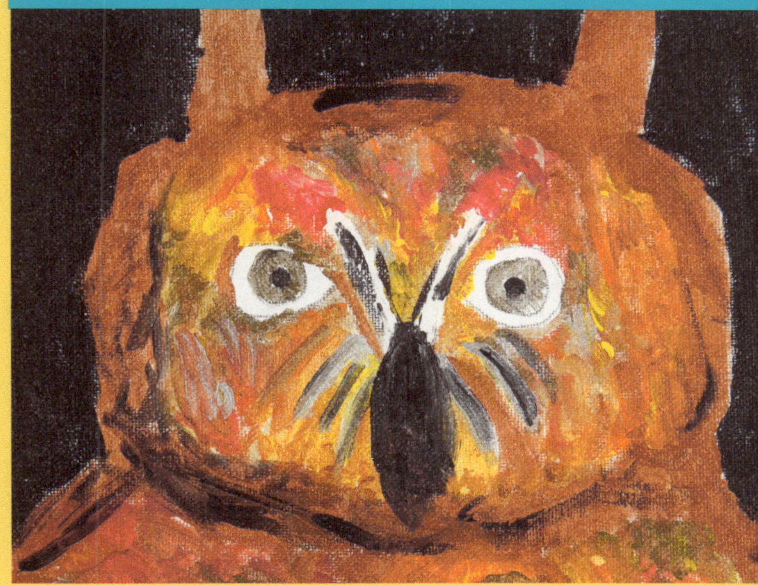

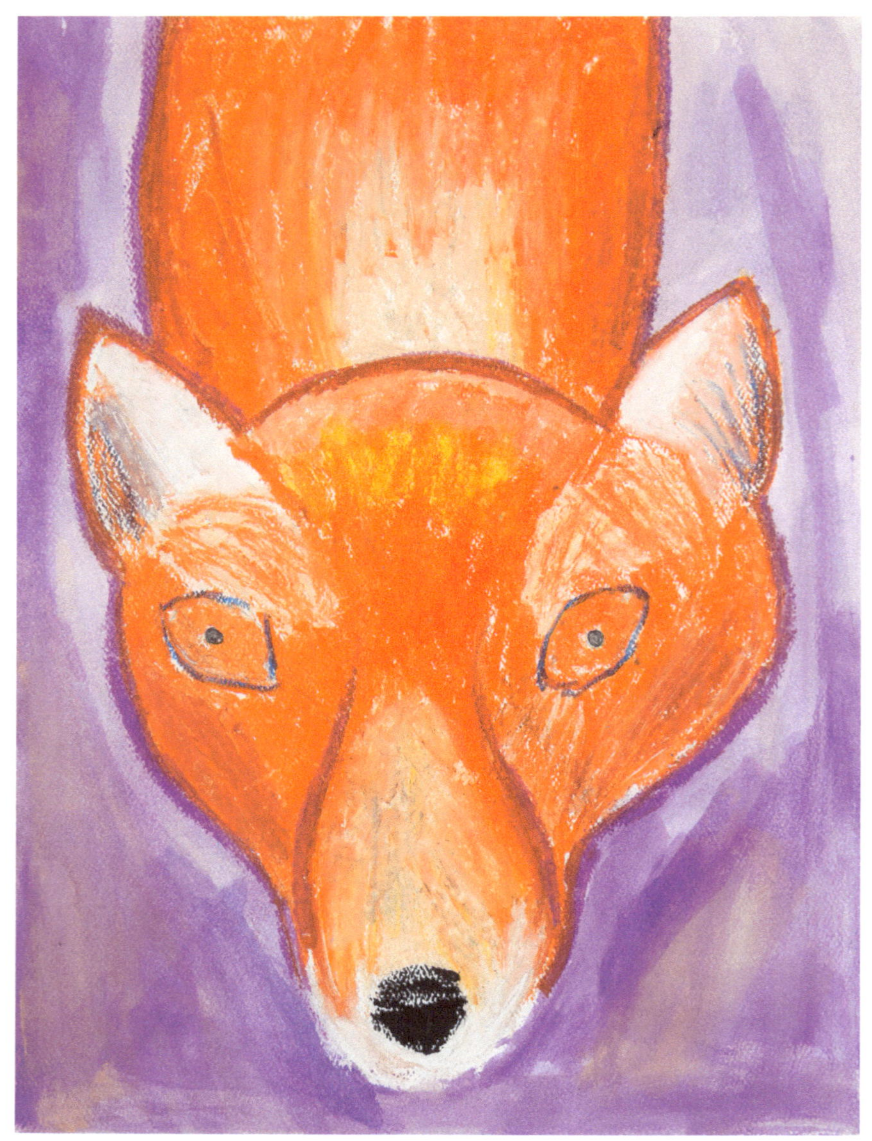

Looking Up
Watercolor and oil pastel, 12 x 9 inches
2015

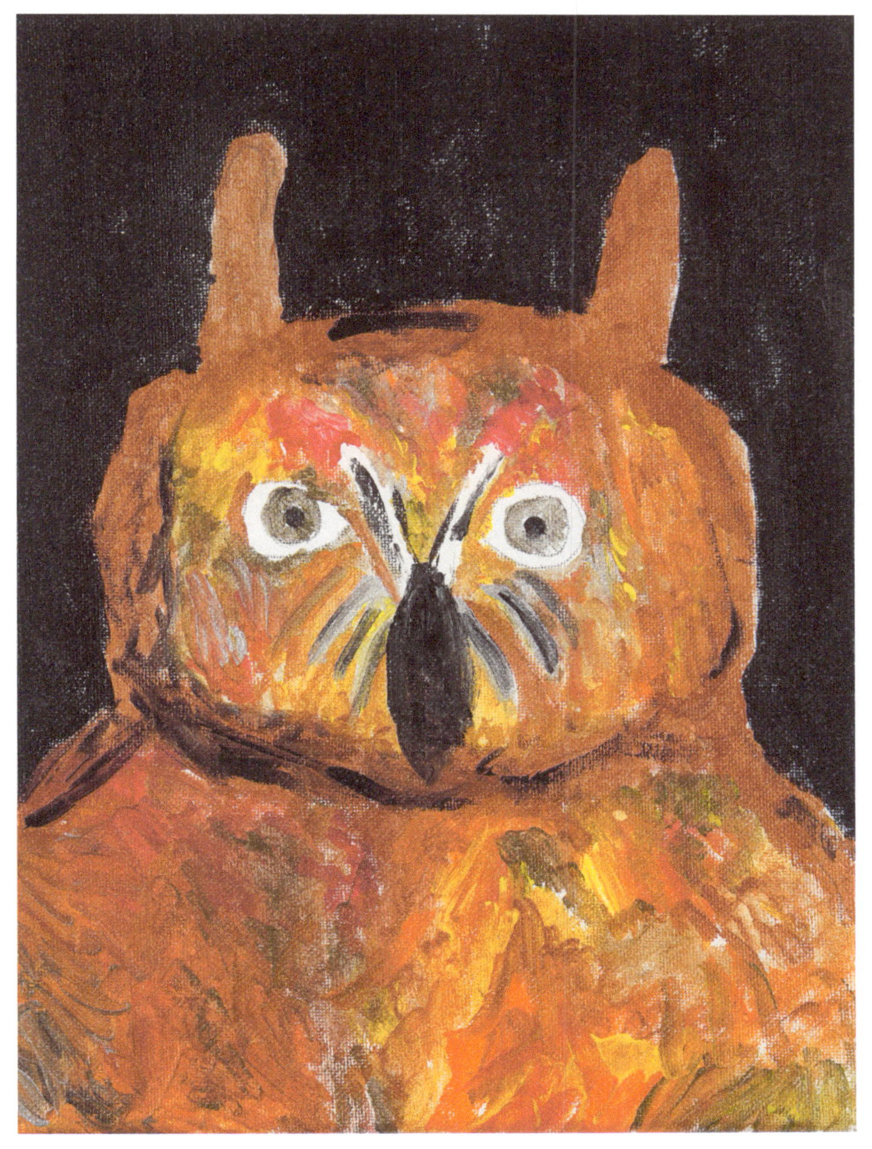

Owl at Night
Acrylic on canvas, 12 x 9 inches
2017

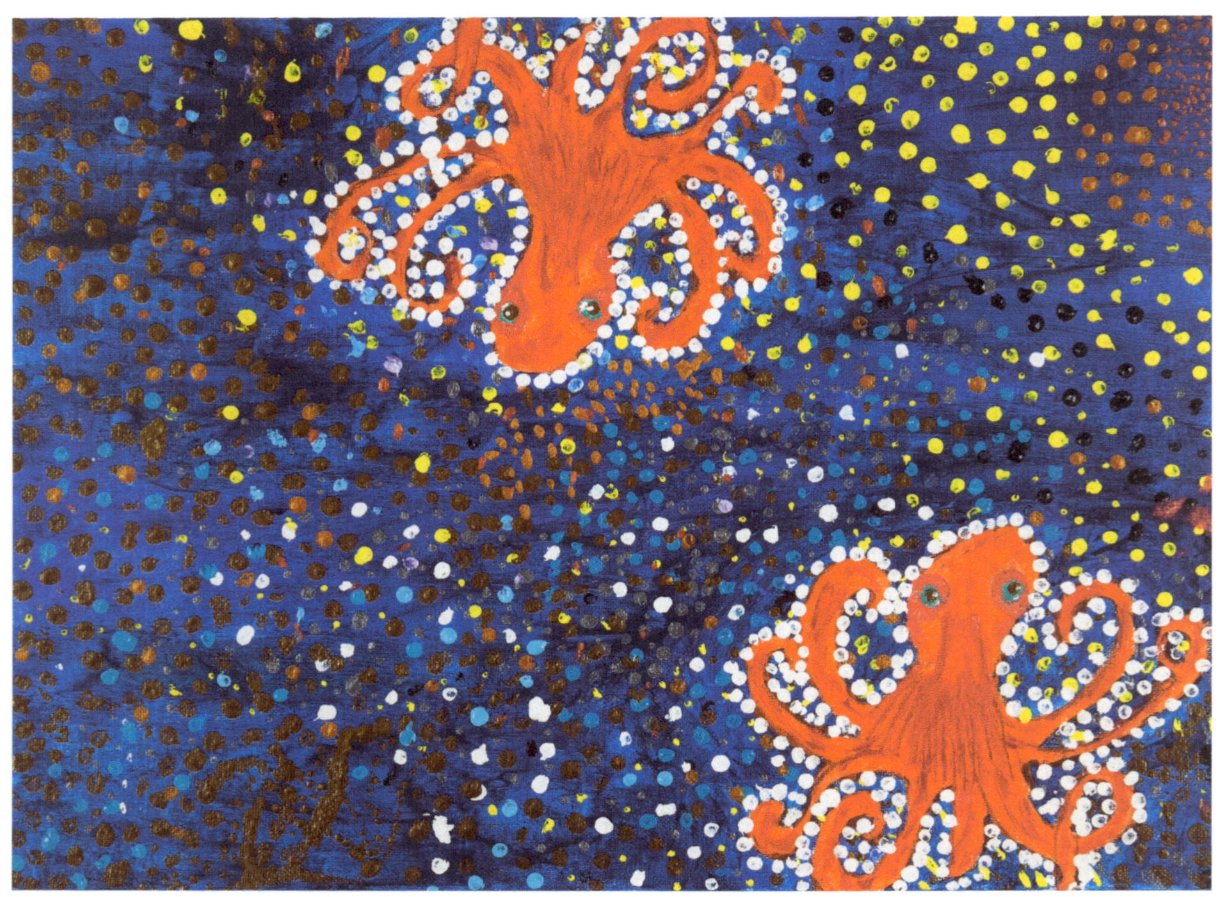

Under the Sea
Acrylic on canvas, 12 x 16 inches
2016

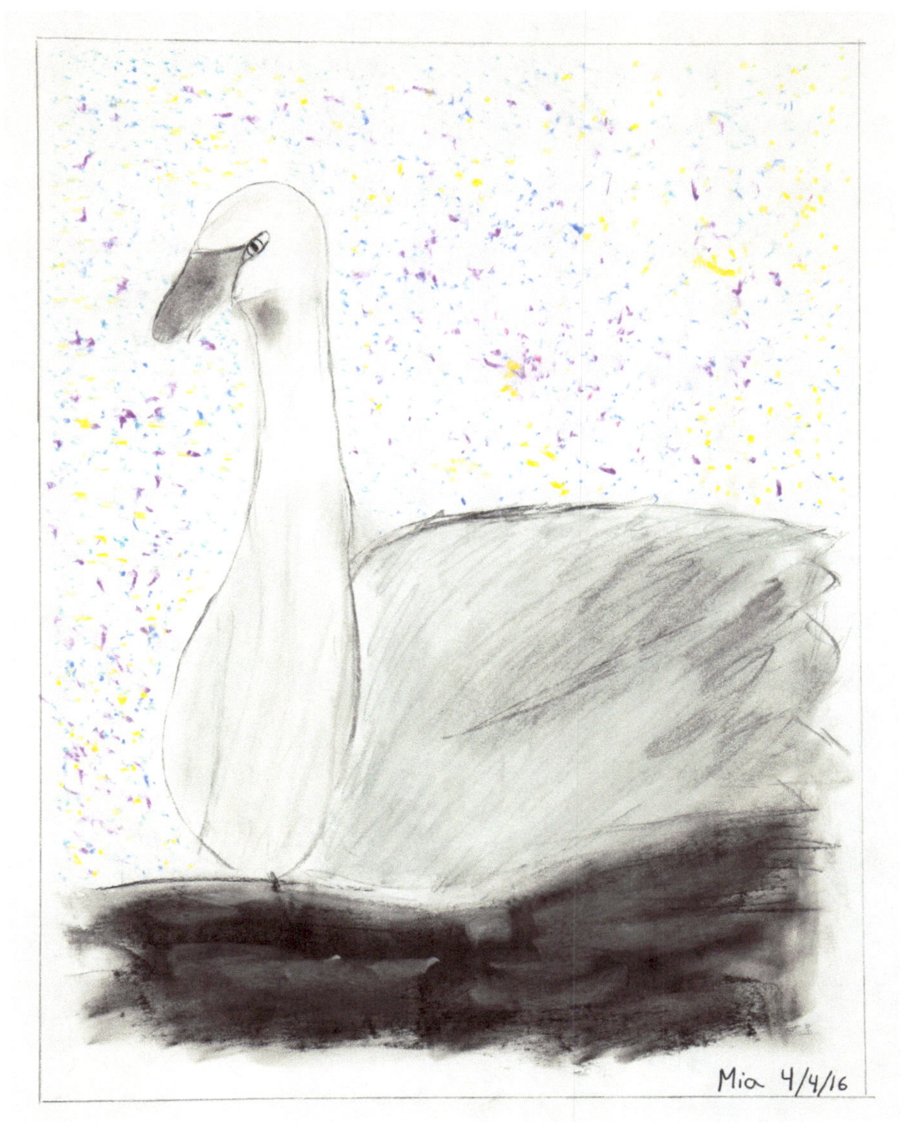

The Swan
Charcoal and oil pastel on paper, 28 x 22.5 inches
2016

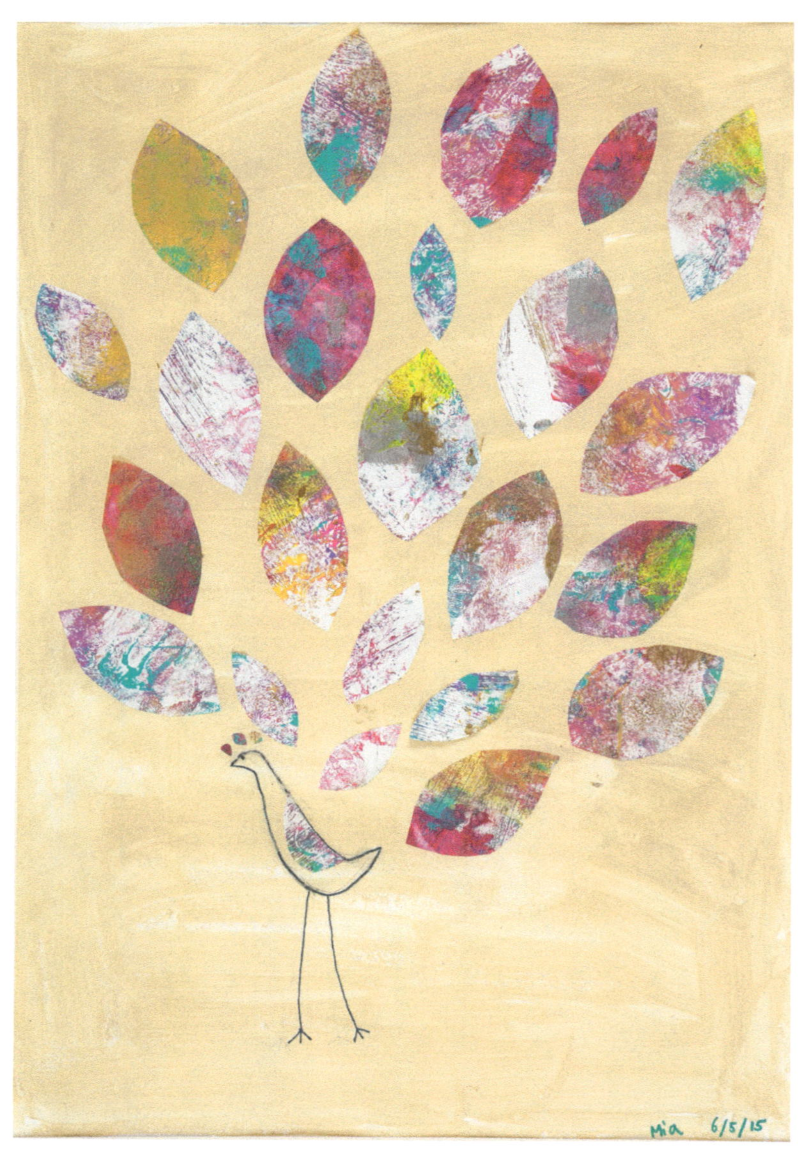

The Peacock
Acrylic on paper, 24 x 16 inches
2015

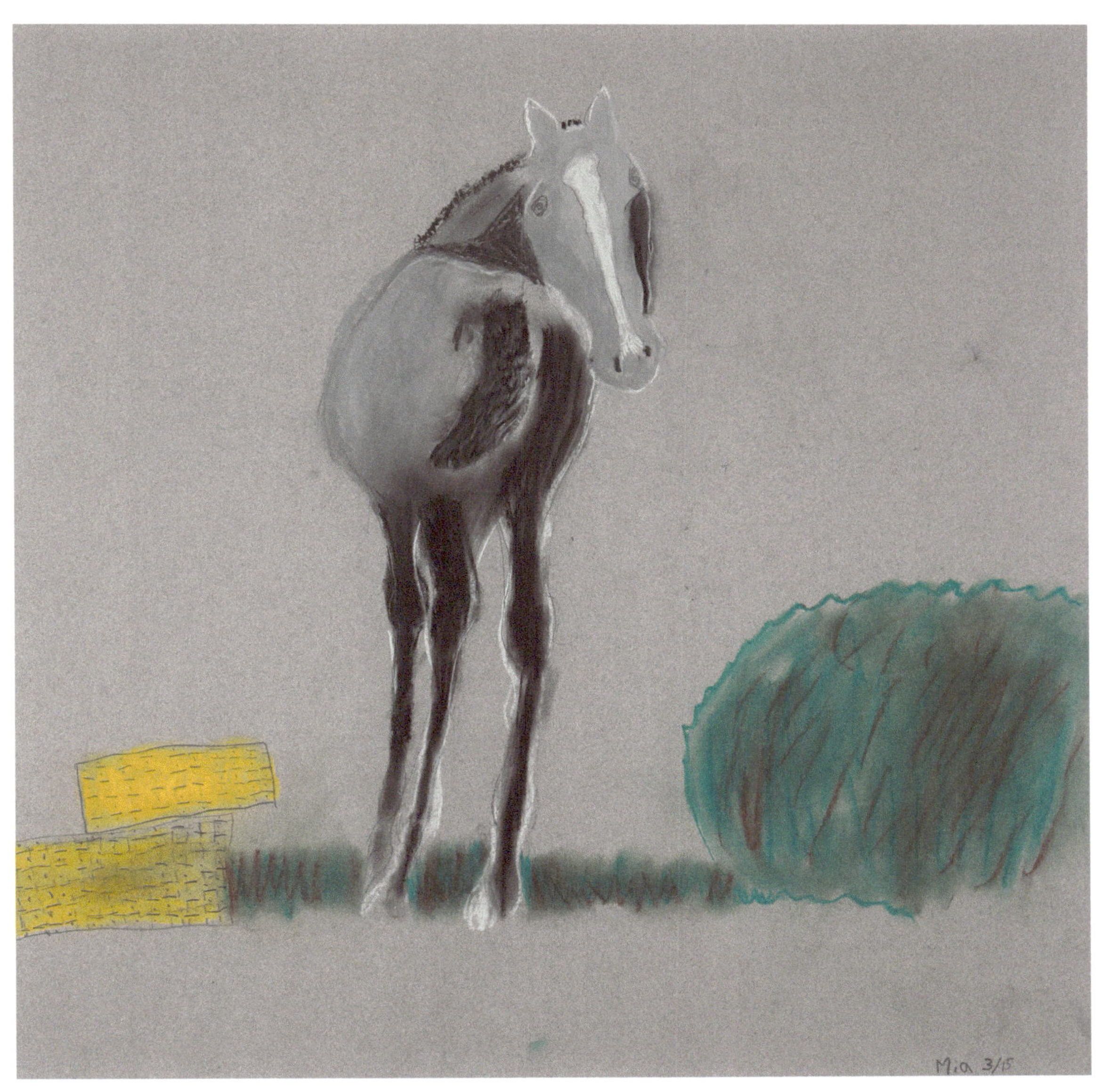

The Horse
Chalk on paper, 18.5 x 18.5 inches
2015

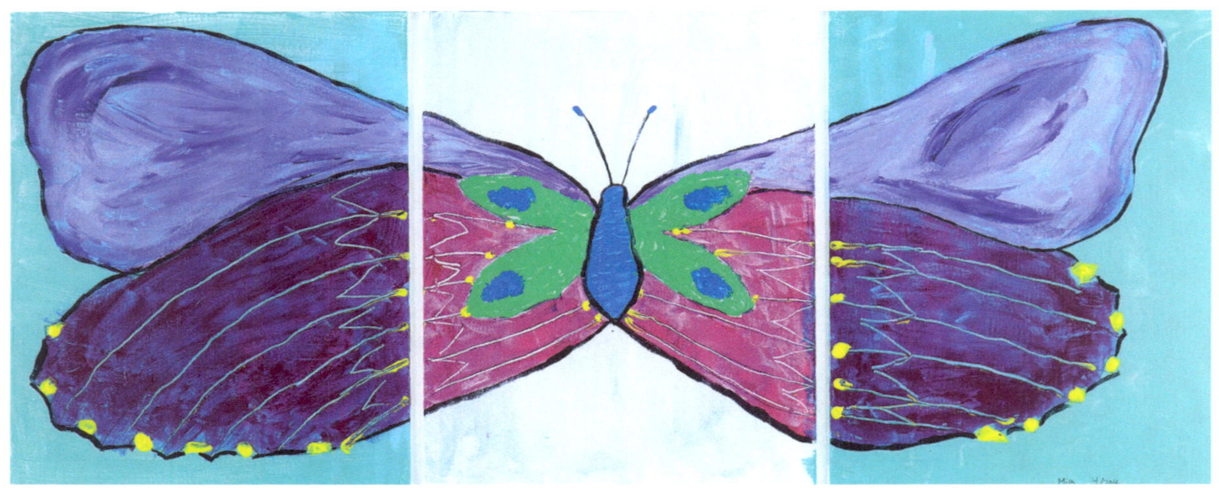

The Butterfly
Acrylic on canvas, 14 x 33.5 inches
2016

Abstract Paintings

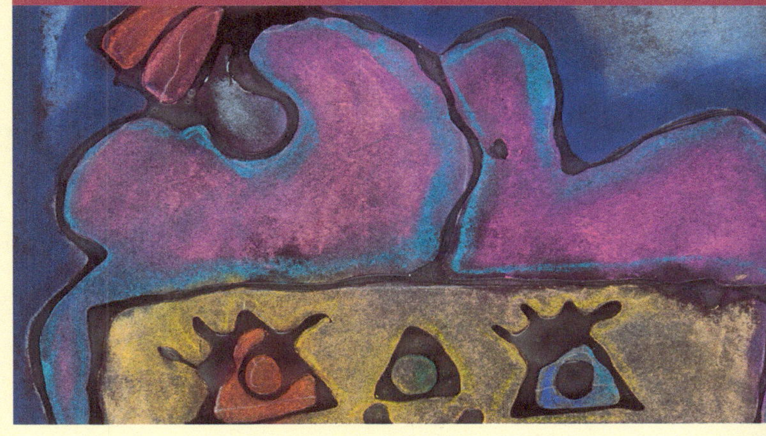

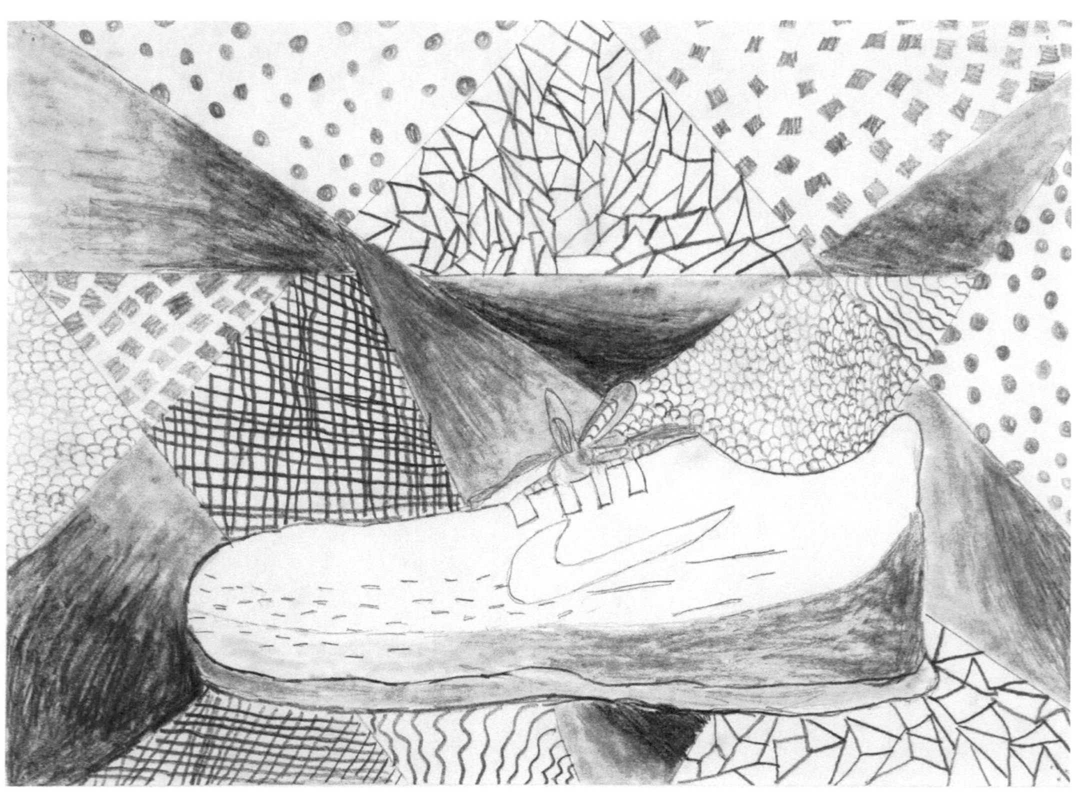

Kicks
Graphite on paper, 9 x 12 inches
2016

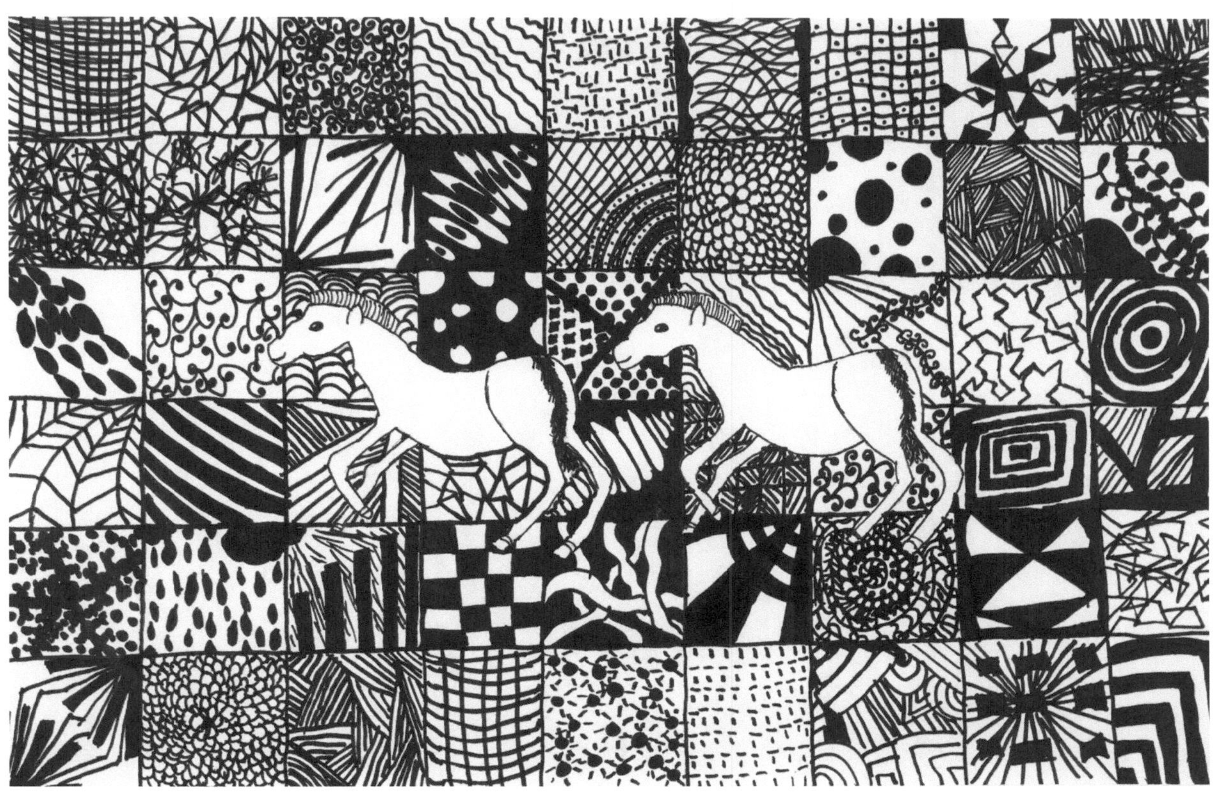

Patterned Trot
Ink on paper, 12 x 18 inches
2016

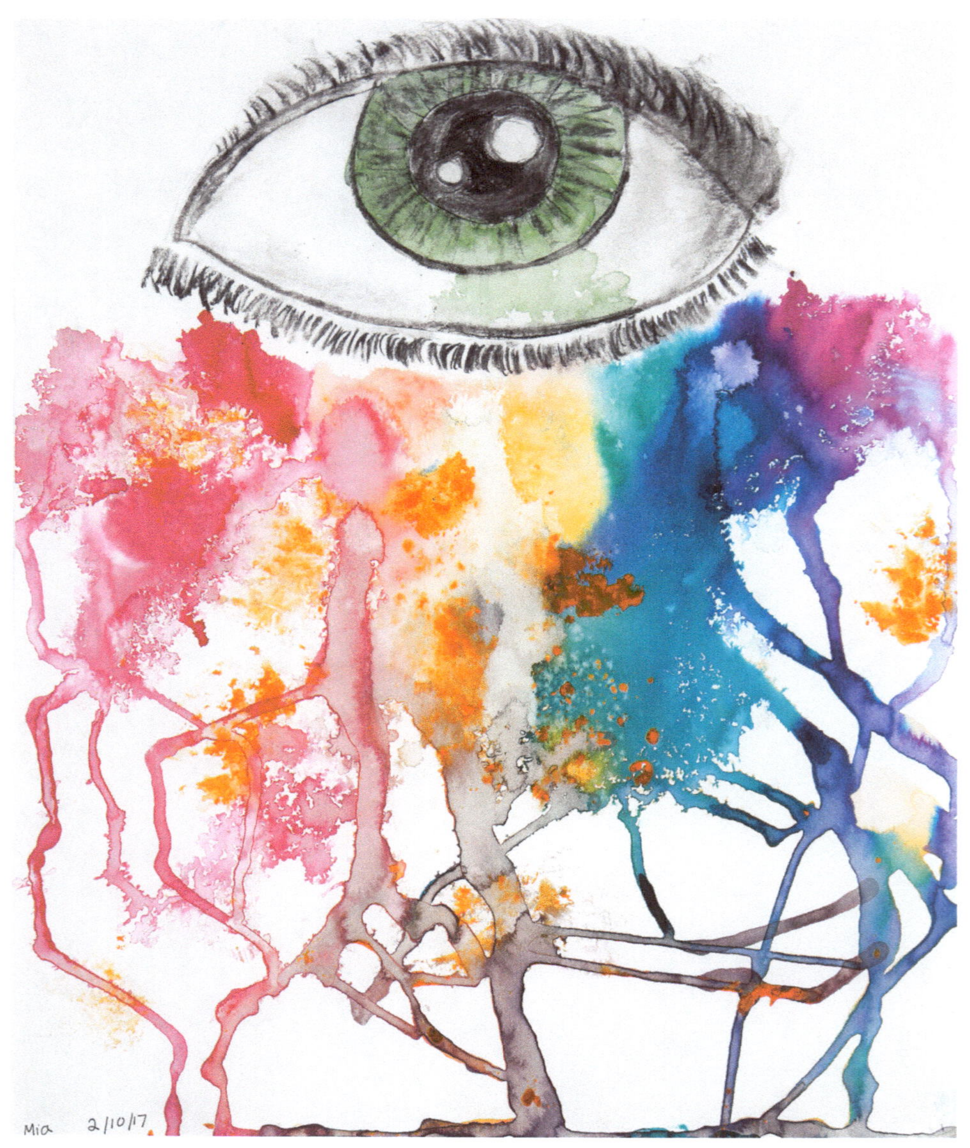

Untitled (green eye)
Ink and charcoal on paper, 17 x 14 inches
2017

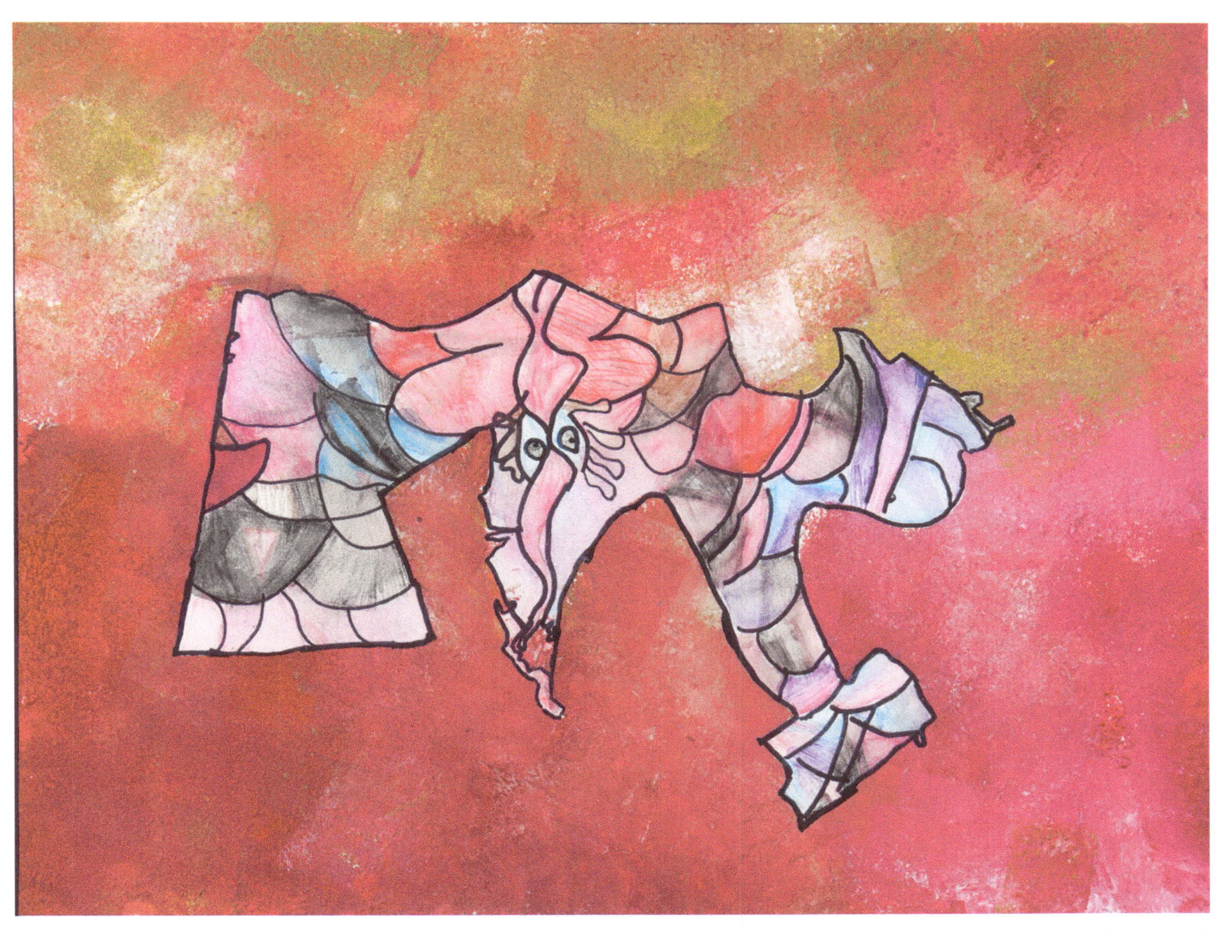

Untitled (bird with red background)
Marker, colored pencil, watercolor, and acrylic on paper, 14 x 18 inches
2012

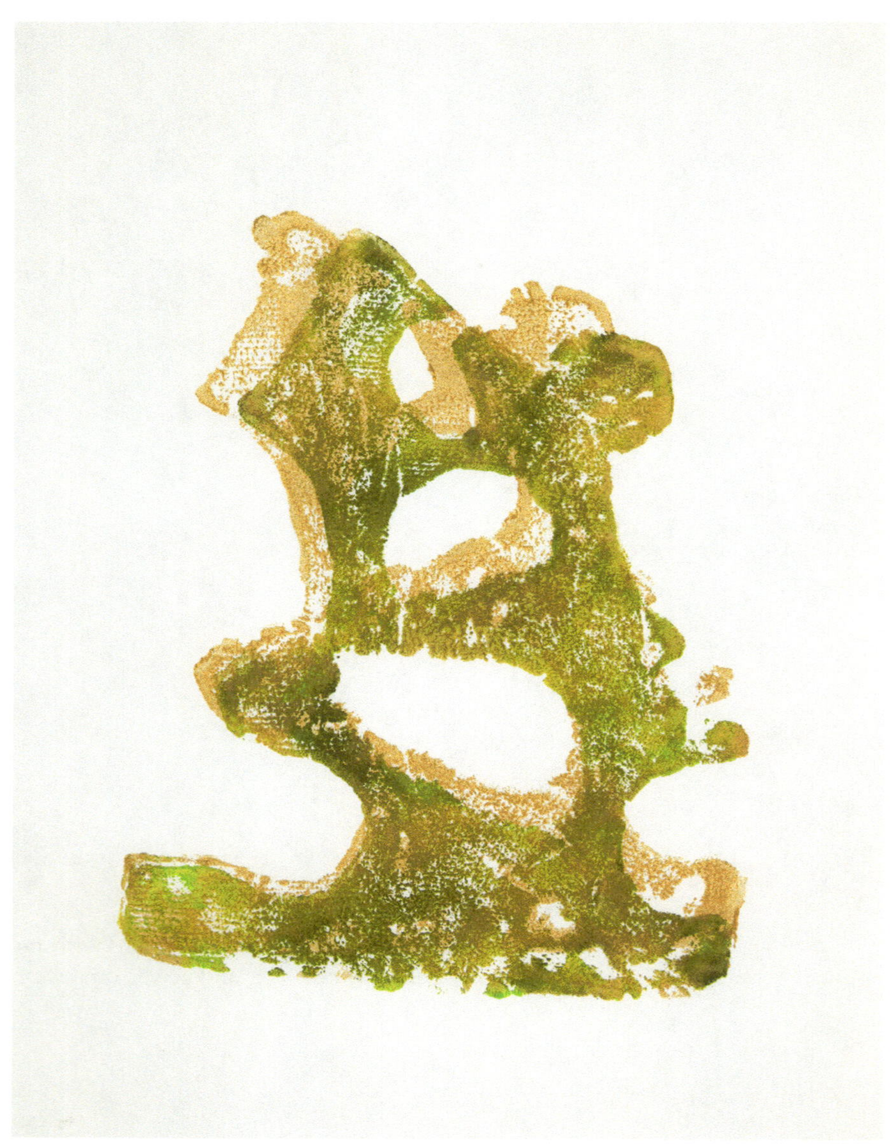

Print I
Acrylic on paper, 30 x 22.5 inches
2016

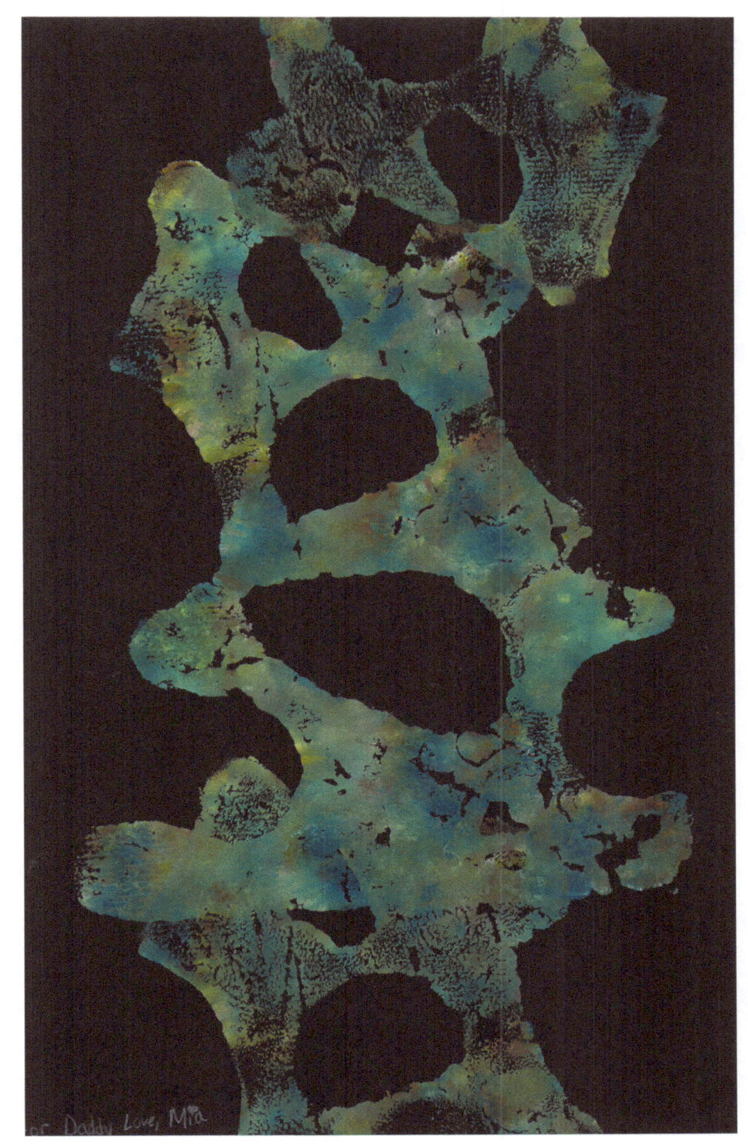

Print II
Acrylic on paper, 22 x 14 inches
2016

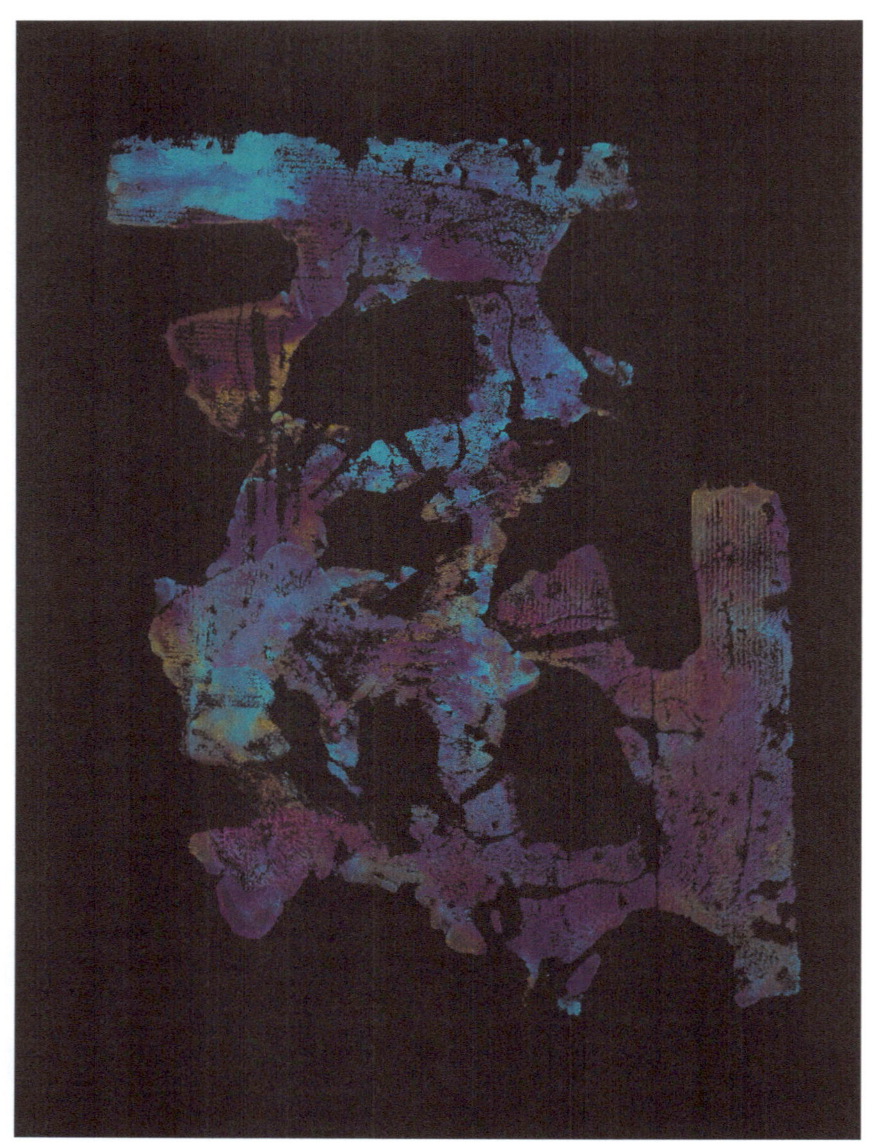

Print III
Acrylic on paper, 28 x 22 inches
2016

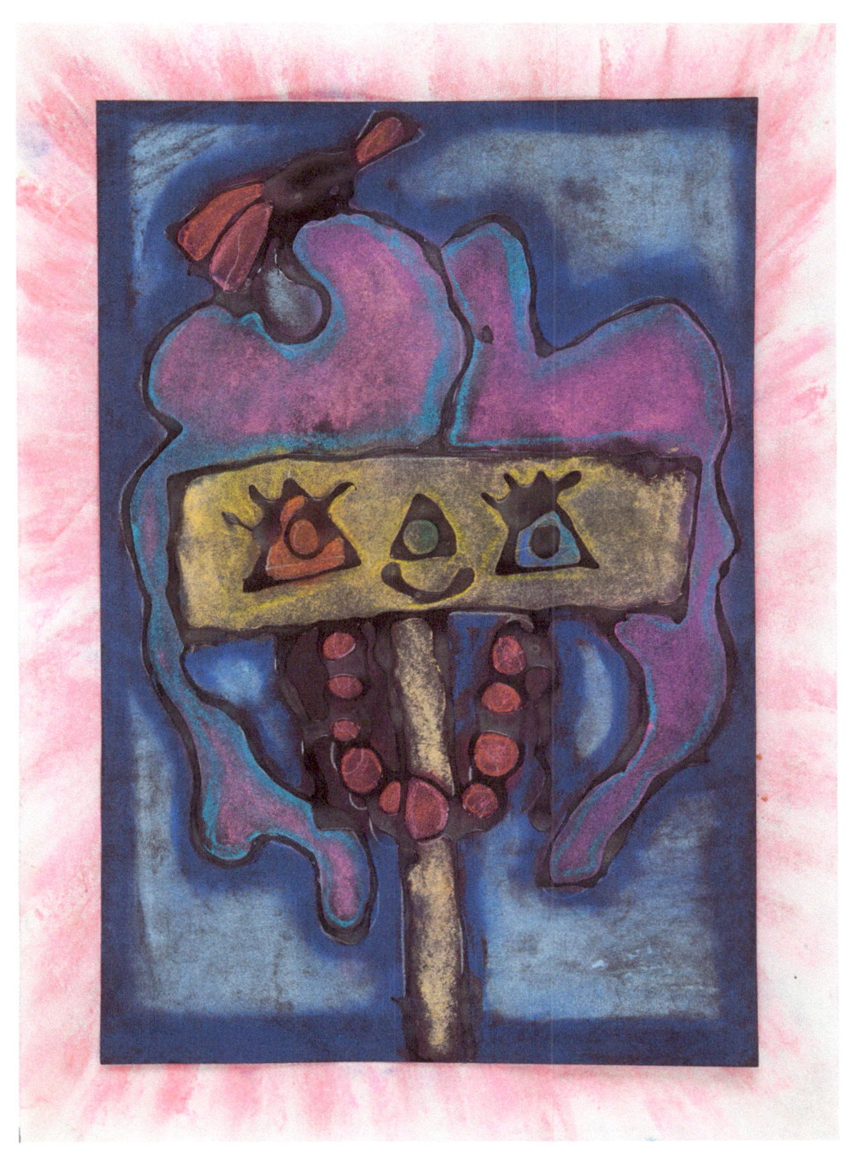

Unique Girl
Glue, chalk, and oil pastel on paper, 21 x 15 inches
2012

Drawings

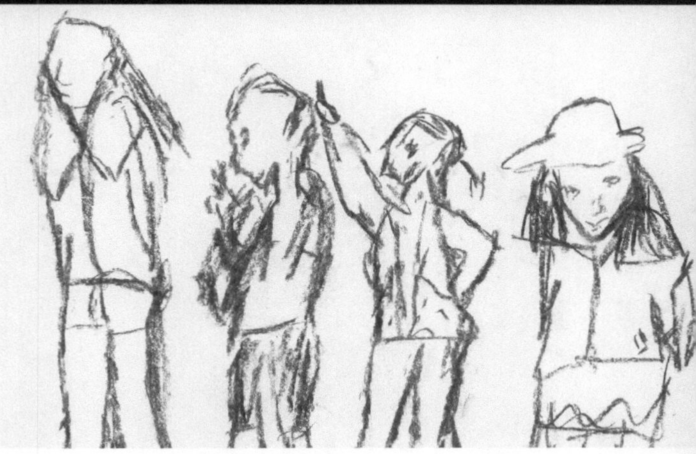

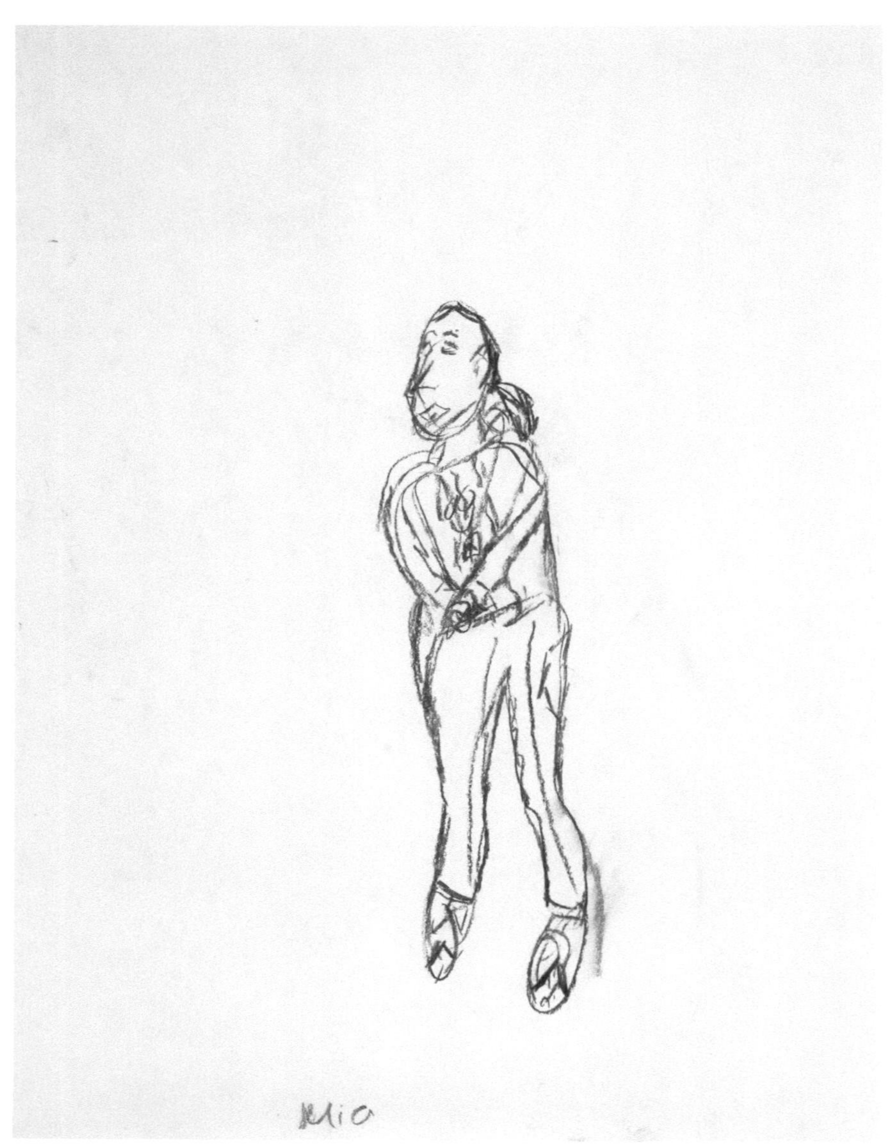

Krista
Charcoal on paper, 24 x 18 inches
2017

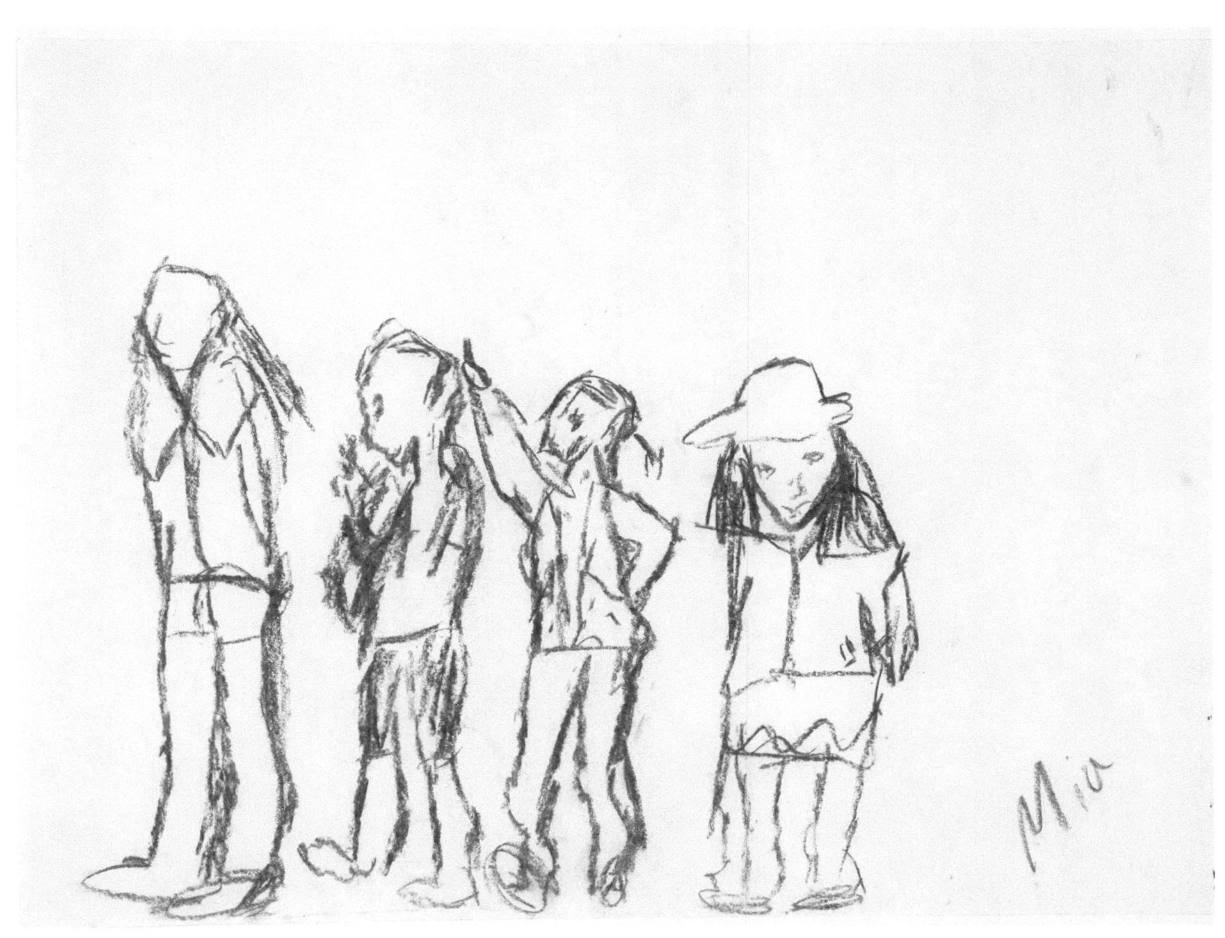

Untitled (four people posing)
Charcoal on paper, 18 x 24 inches
2017

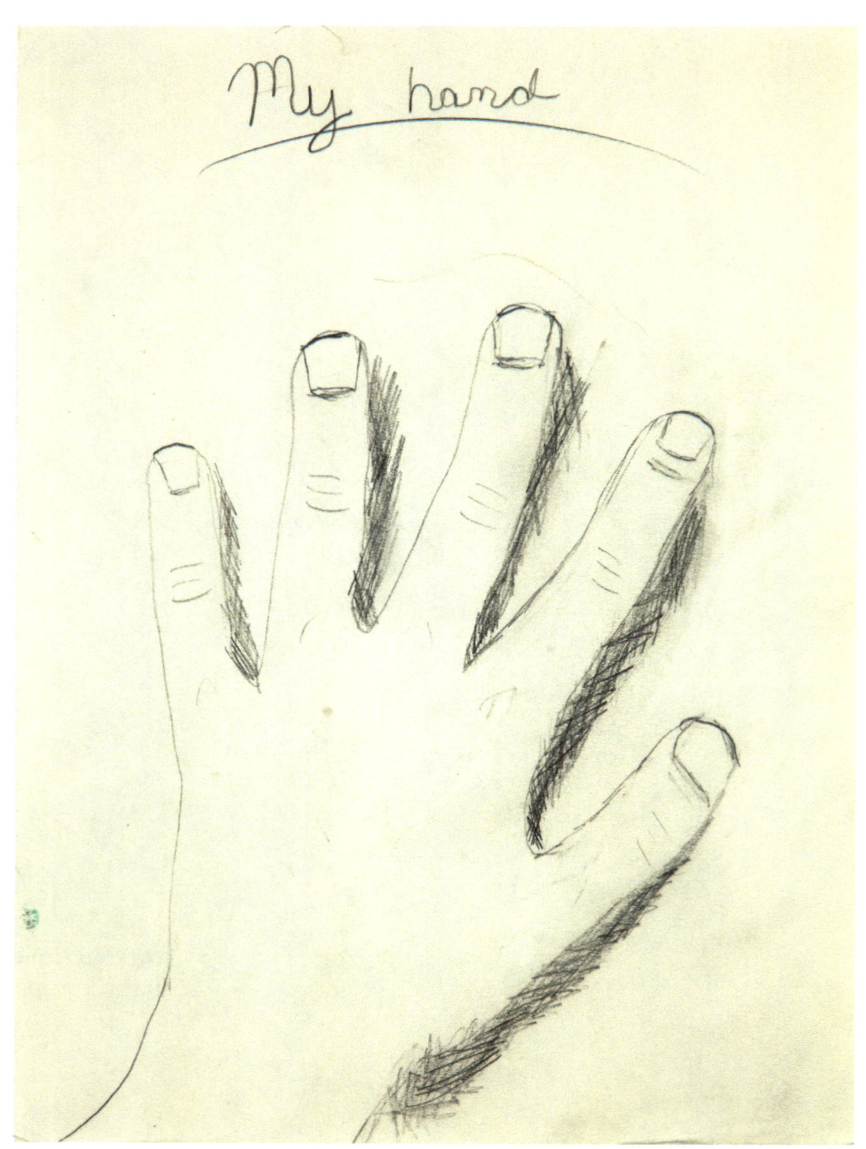

My Hand
Graphite on paper, 8 x 6 inches
2017

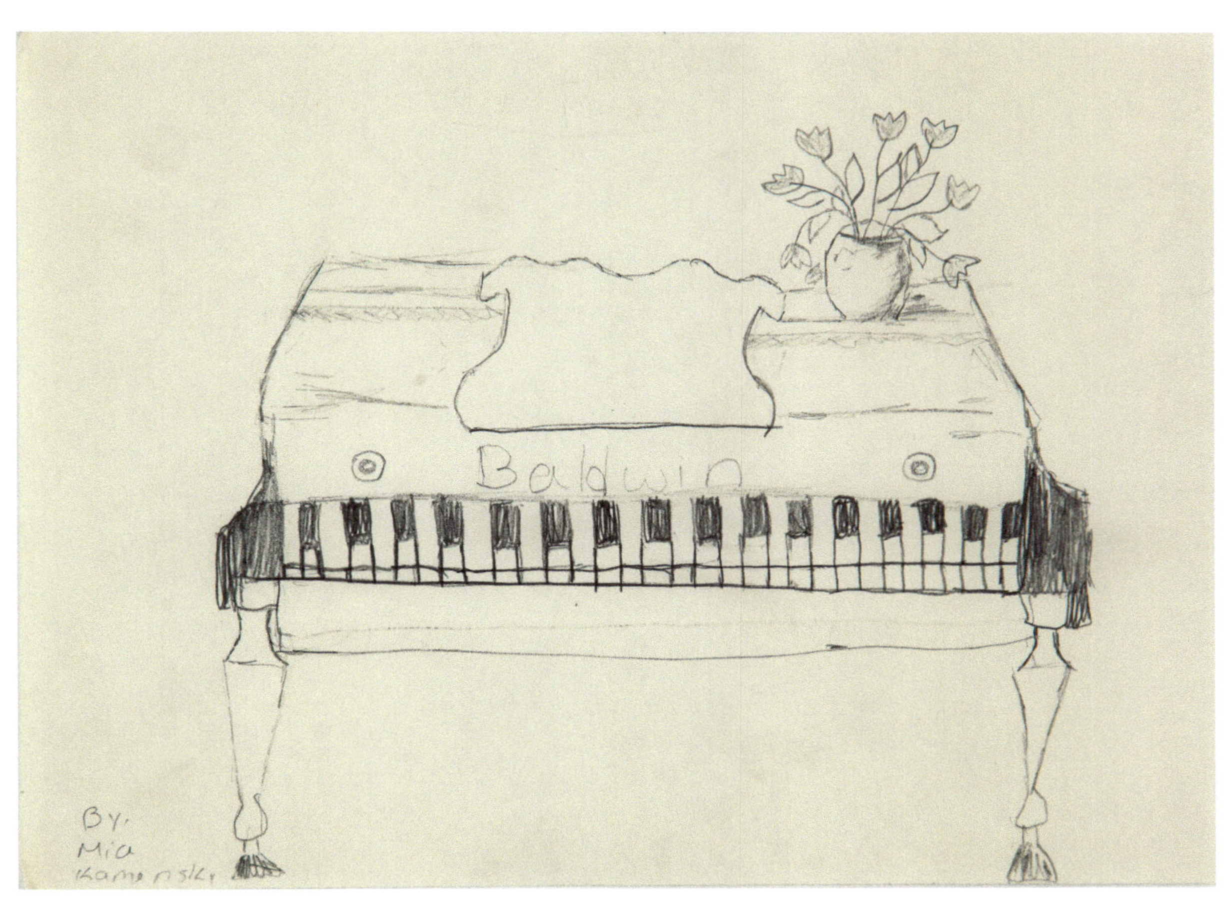

My Piano
Graphite on paper, 6 x 8 inches
2017

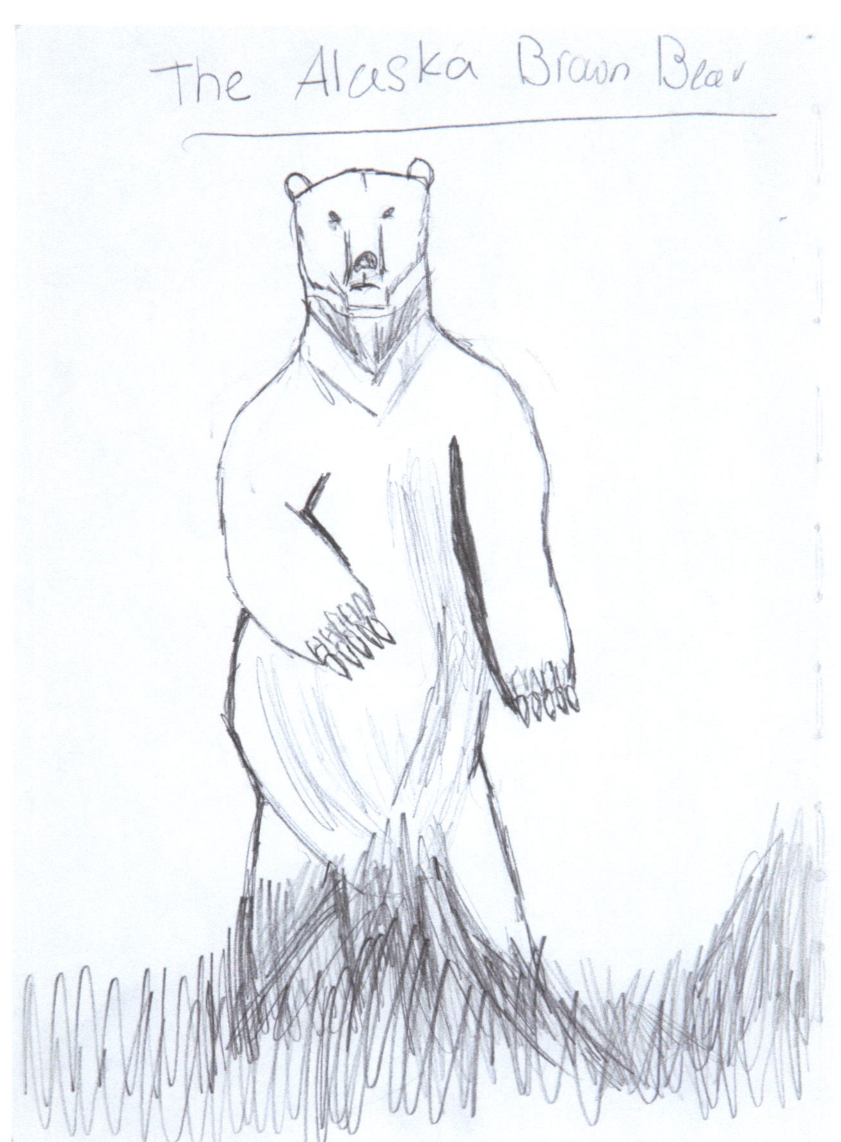

The Alaska Brown Bear
Graphite on paper, 10 x 7 inches
2017

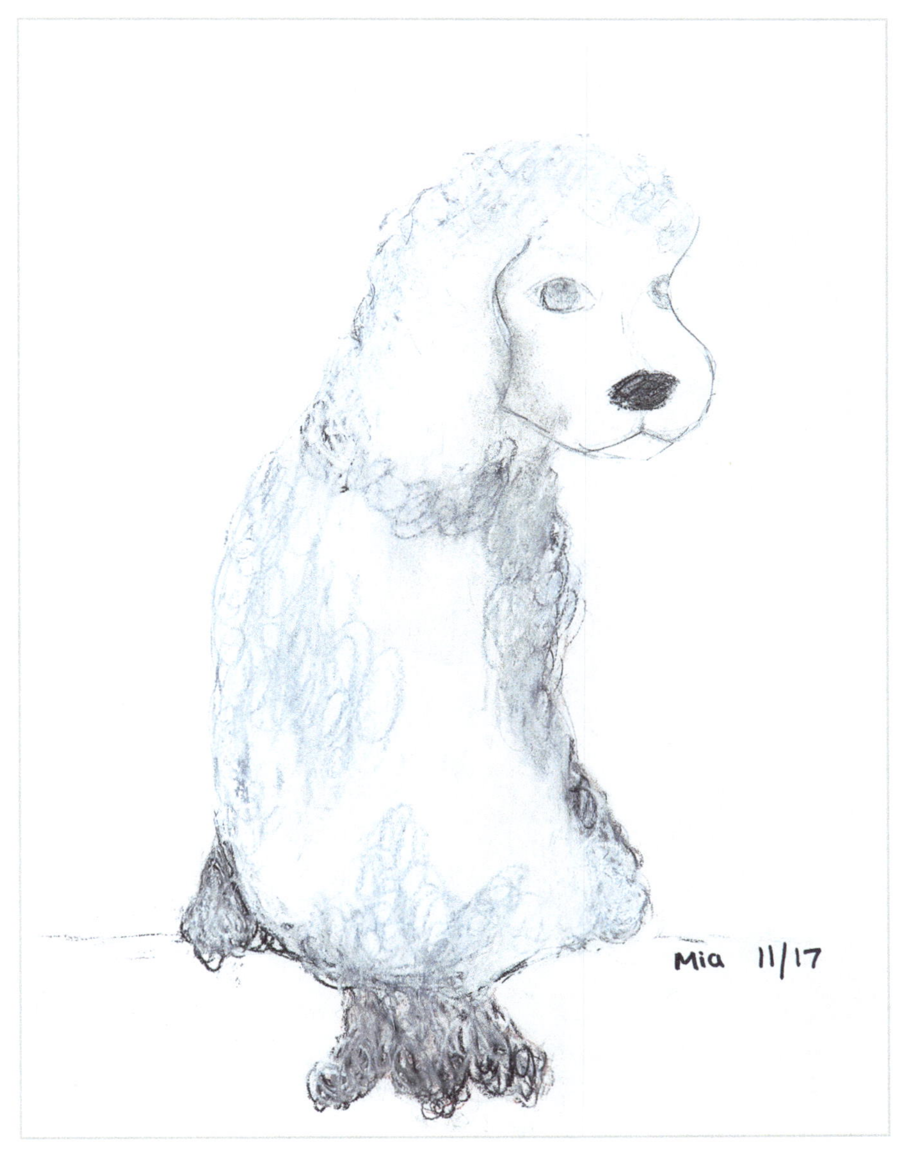

Ollie
Graphite, chalk, charcoal on paper, 17 x 14 inches
2017

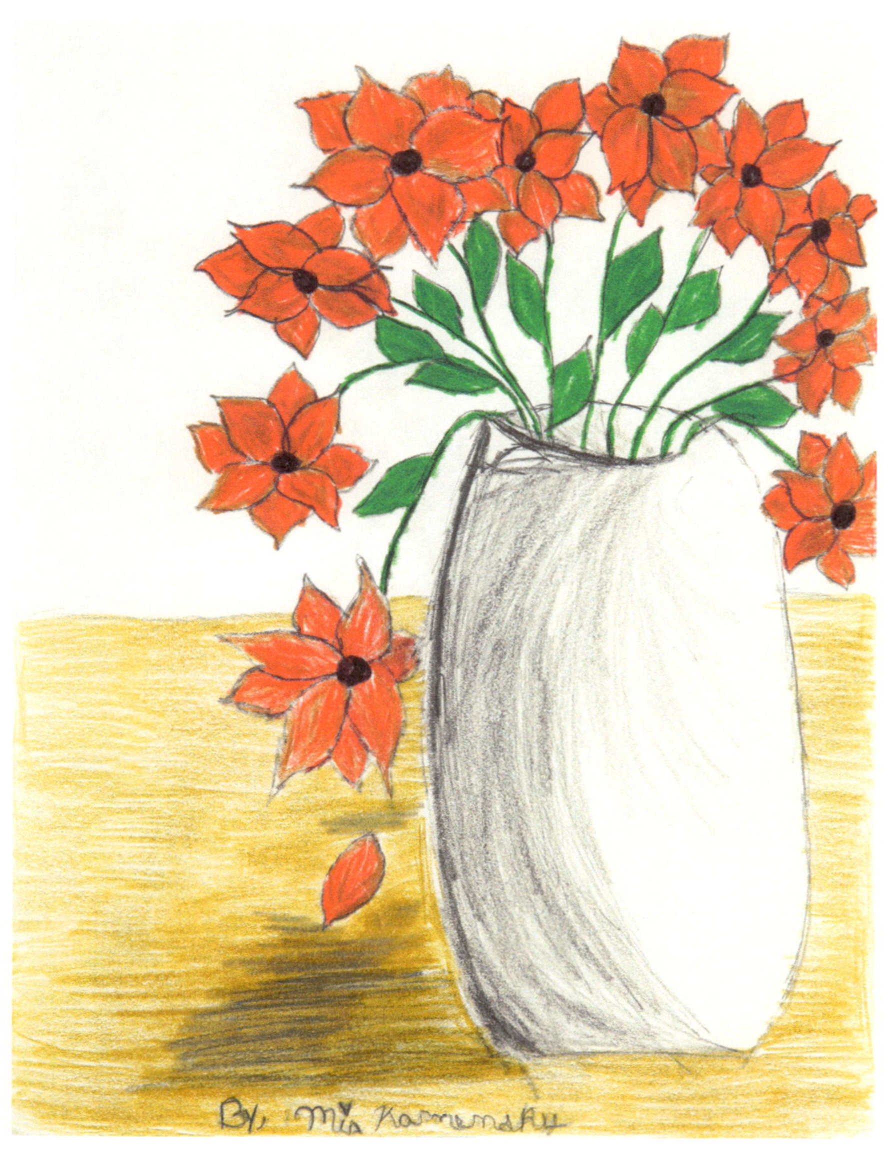

Bouquet
Graphite and colored pencil on paper, 8 x 6 inches
2017

Early Paintings

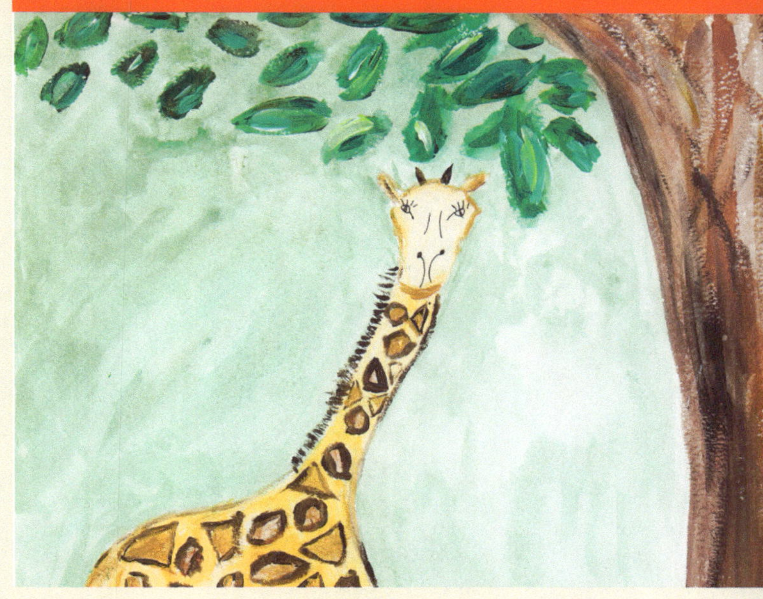

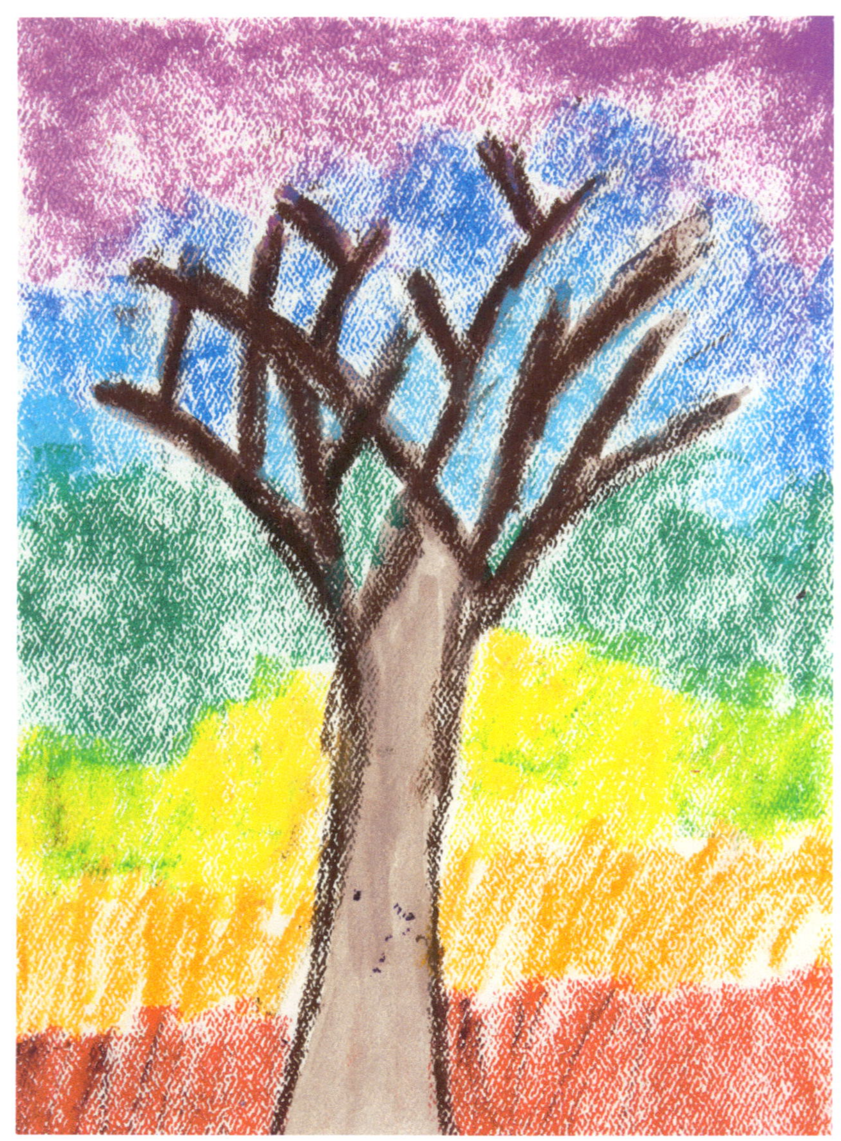

Rainbow Tree
Oil pastel and watercolor on paper, 11 x 8 inches
2013

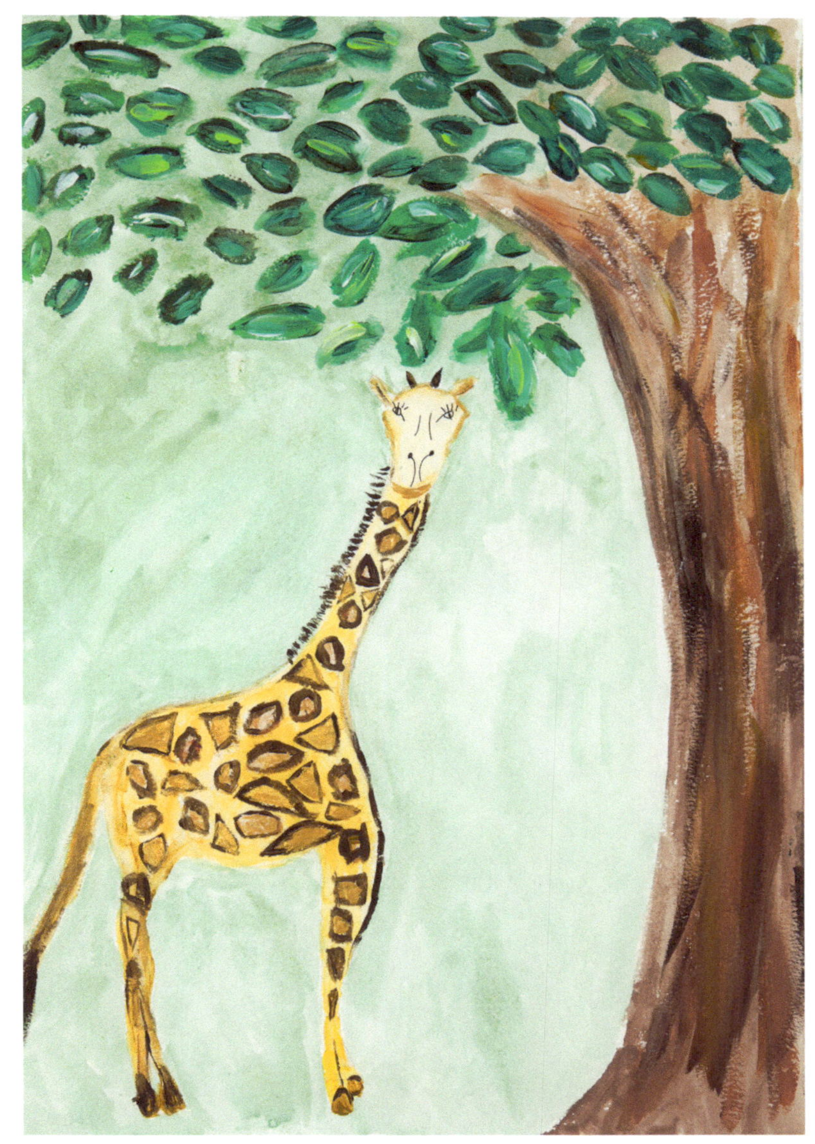

Giraffe
Acrylic and watercolor on paper, 22 x 15 inches
2014

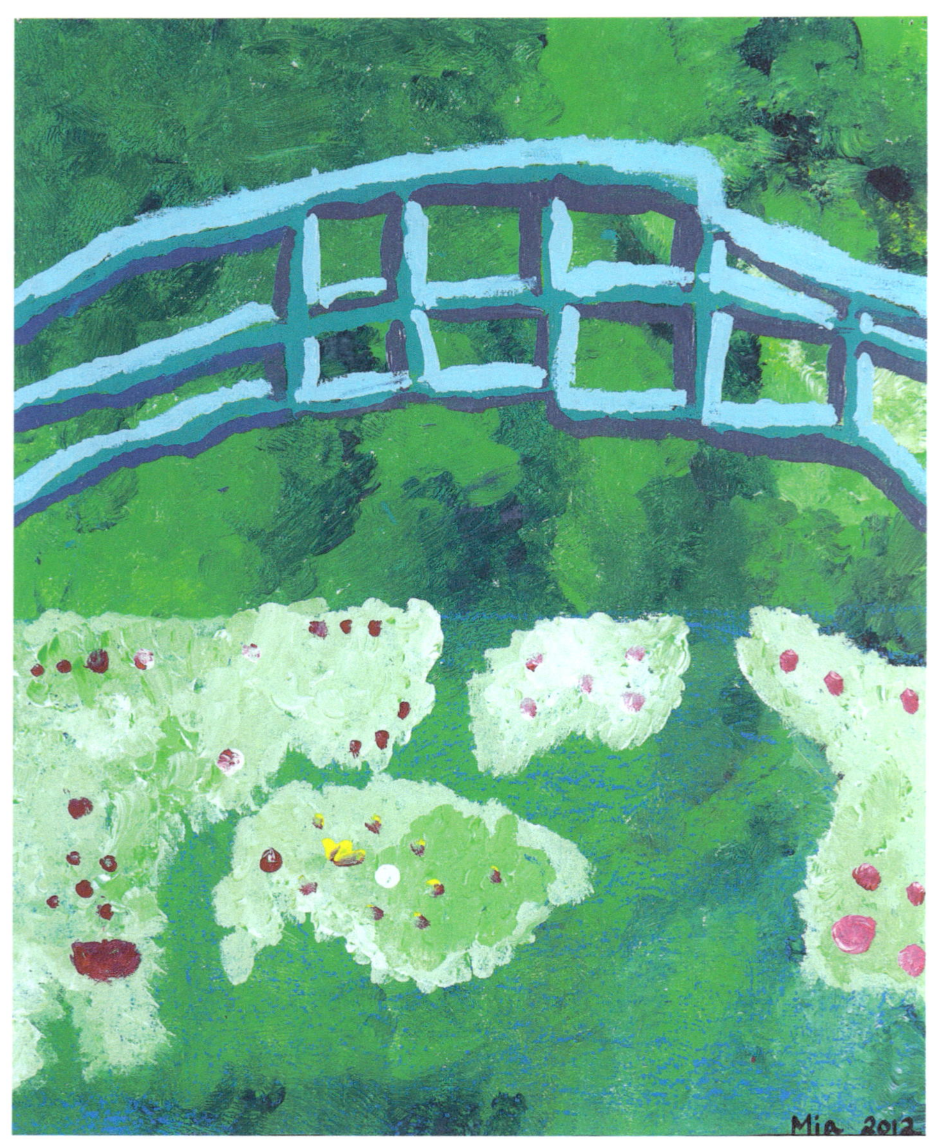

Monet's Bridge
Acrylic on canvas, 19 x 15.5 inches
2012

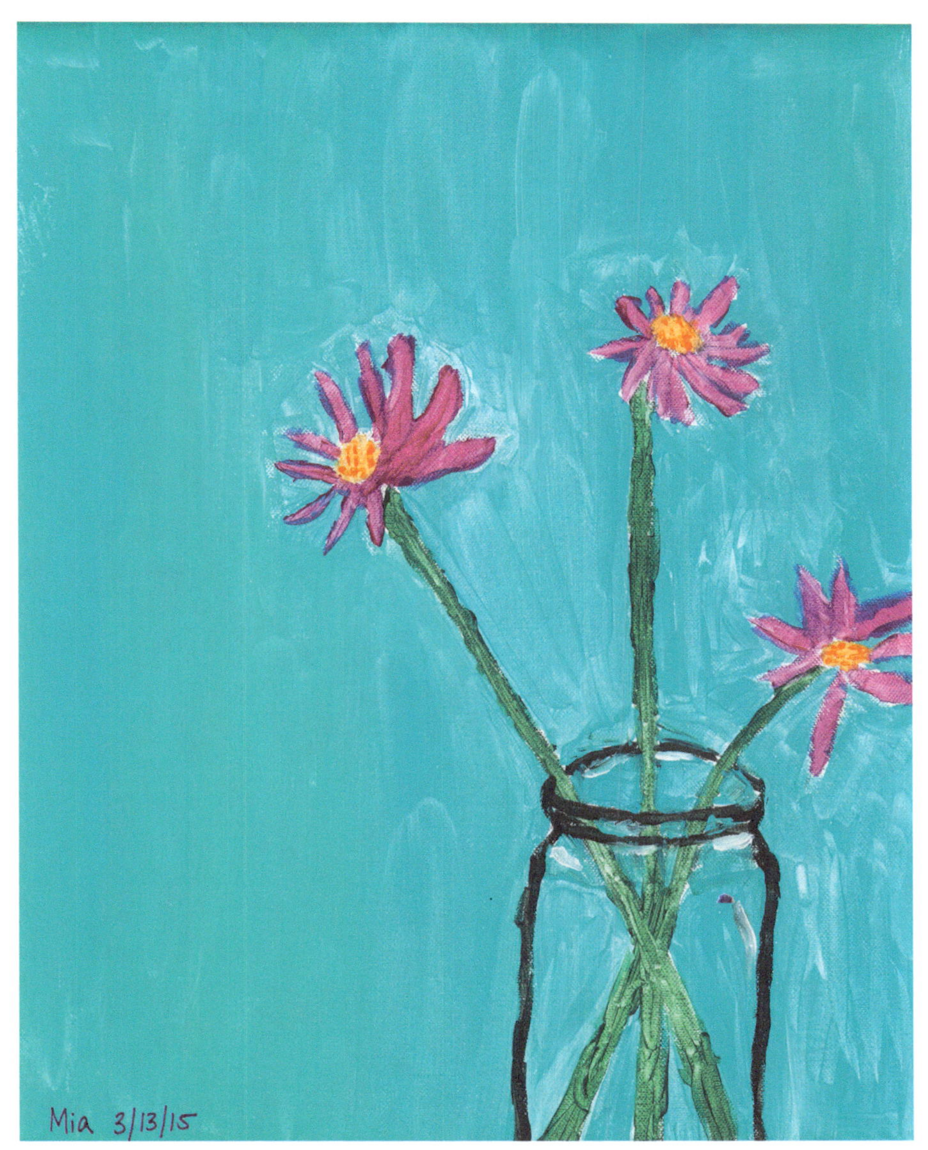

Flowers on Turquoise Ground
Acrylic on canvas, 20 x 16 inches
2015

Index of Color Plates

Index of Color Plates

www.ingramcontent.com/pod-product-compliance
Lightning Source LLC
LaVergne TN
LVHW070134110826
845147LV00002B/246

9780983076292